A DIFFERENT
SHADE OF GREEN

D1602771

A DIFFERENT SHADE OF GREEN

*A Biblical Approach to Environmentalism
and the Dominion Mandate*

Gordon Wilson

canonpress
Moscow, Idaho

Gordon Wilson, *A Different Shade of Green:*
A Biblical Approach to Environmentalism and the Dominion Mandate
Copyright © 2019 by Gordon Wilson
Published by Canon Press
P. O. Box 8729, Moscow, Idaho 83843
800-488-2034 | www.canonpress.com

Cover design by James Engerbretson. Interior design by Valerie Anne Bost.
Illustrations by Forrest Dickison, and taken with permission from *The Riot
and the Dance: Foundational Biology* by Gordon Wilson (Canon Press, 2014).
Printed in the United States of America

Library of Congress Cataloging-in-Publication Data:
Wilson, Gordon L., 1961- author.
A different shade of green : a biblical approach to environmentalism and
the dominion mandate /
   Gordon Wilson.
Biodiversity and the dominion mandate
Moscow, Idaho : Canon Press, [2019]
LCCN 2019011429 | ISBN 9781947644571 (pbk.)
LCSH: Biodiversity--Religious aspects. | Biodiversity
   conservation--Religious aspects.
Classification: LCC QH541.15.B56 W5525 2019 | DDC 333.95/16--dc23
LC record available at https://lccn.loc.gov/2019011429

19 20 21 22 23 24 25   10 9 8 7 6 5 4 3 2 1

To my four children,

Brooke, Dane, Mallory, and Heather,

who explored and relished the great outdoors

while catching reptiles and amphibians with me.

CONTENTS

Foreword: A Different Shade of Uncle   **ix**

Part 1: Biblical Reasons for Wise Dominion   **1**

1. From Brown to Green   **3**

2. The Foundation for Conservation   **15**

3. Food . . . and Other Good Stuff   **23**

4. The Dominion Mandate: He Commanded Us to .
   Care for It   **29**

5. Maintaining the Created Diversity   **37**

6. A Christian View of Animal Care   **45**

7. Creation's Declaration of God's Care, Glory, and
   Wisdom   **51**

Part 2: Practical Reasons for Wise Dominion   **57**

8. Creation: Our Life Support System   **59**

9. Creation: The Great Recycler   **67**

10. Biodiversity's Benefits   **81**

Part 3: Problems and Solutions   **95**

11. Christianity Is the Solution, Not the Problem   **97**

12. Environmental Issues and the Christian   **113**

13. Root Causes, Root Solutions to Environmental
    Problems   **155**

14. How Shall We Now Live?   **181**

Further Reading   **187**

Acknowledgments   **189**

FOREWORD:
A DIFFERENT SHADE OF UNCLE

UNCLE GORDON, GORDO, DR. WILSON...
my beloved uncle has worn all of these titles with pride.
When I was young, he was the energetic, outdoorsy
Wilson who would take me frog catching, bug collecting,
nature-doc watching, and even on one disappointing but
enlightening occasion, fossil digging. (I wanted dinosaurs
where only leaves and the very rare fish had been trapped.)

His influence on me has been significant in ways that
I cannot fully process. The way I relate to any old ant on
my shoe has been fundamentally shaped by my uncle's
deep, contagious affection for every single creeping and
crawling thing God has created for us, with an especial
love for the often overlooked underdogs, those common
creatures he so fondly calls "little brown jobs." They,

despite not having a mating dance to match the birds of paradise, are just as miraculous, just as divinely crafted, and just as much part of the canon of natural revelation as the rare and the bizarre.

When I was choosing a graduate school, I headed across the continent to be close to my uncle and his family and reacquaint myself with his contagious sparkle in the great outdoors. When I was married and moved back to Idaho to raise my own children, I began a campaign to bring Uncle Gordon's clan back as well. Eventually, we talked the owner of the house next door into selling and landed ourselves some of the best neighbors money can't possibly buy. When my eldest was headed into kindergarten, his Great-Uncle Gordon took him tromping down some railroad tracks beside the Snake River where they captured a young gopher snake. That snake was promptly named Jack and became a member of our family for the next decade. One year in, when Jack was ill and dying, it was Uncle Gordon who sat on the porch with us and taught us how to force-feed the little guy tiny balls of raw hamburger, eventually nursing him back to full health. Jack now rests beneath a marked grave in our side yard, awaiting the resurrection. Dave, a robust black-headed python, carries the snake torch in our family these days.

Uncle Gordon's influence is even why two (now massive) tortoises have been grazing in my yard for ten years. My kids can tell you, I struggle to say no to reptiles.

But I wasn't just able to chase creatures with Uncle Gordon in my childhood. As a filmmaker directing *The Riot and The Dance,* named after his Biology text, I've been blessed to pursue cobras and leopards and elephants with him in wild and distant places. I, and a few other humans, shared several uncaged hours with Uncle Gordon and a couple dozen circling sharks three miles off the coast of Oahu. And I can tell you, when Uncle Gordon gets seasick and chucks in sharky water, he doesn't get any less cheerful, even if the sharks and I do.

This book is another aspect of the life of Gordon Wilson, the part where he ponders big issues and communicates his conclusions in down-to-earth images and prose, like a highly educated Pooh Bear. I've spent a lot of time with that version of Gordon as well, mostly on porches and in living rooms, with both of us sniffing at the smell of the next beloved season coming our way and sipping on seasonally appropriate drinks as metaphors and counter-arguments slowly take shape in our minds. That Gordon Wilson is a fantastic conversation partner and just as much fun as the man who used to bring snakes over to the house for my sisters and I to hold. I hope you enjoy his thoughts and conversation as much as I do, and I look forward to more sessions of my own, seated on his new porch in the country, on the land which I developed so that we could once again be neighbors. On land which I developed entirely without consulting any ecologists whatsoever . . . on which he hopes to grow native plants and where I hope to plant a deciduous wood completely inappropriate to the region. And where we will both toast any critters that we see (especially the little brown jobs).

N.D. WILSON
SUMMER 2019

PART 1: BIBLICAL REASONS FOR WISE DOMINION

1. FROM BROWN TO GREEN: A SPECTRUM OF ATTITUDES HELD BY CHRISTIANS ON THE ENVIRONMENT

So fallen man has dominion over nature, but he uses it wrongly.
The Christian is called upon to exhibit this dominion, but to
exhibit it rightly: Treating the thing as having value in itself,
exercising dominion without being destructive.

FRANCIS A. SCHAEFFER[1]

AS THE OUTDOOR HUMORIST PATRICK
McManus once wrote (very aptly, I might add), "Everyone
now points firmly and with great authority in a different
direction . . . The most forceful personality in the group
gets his way . . . The most forceful personality usually

1. Francis A. Schaeffer and Udo W. Middelmann, *Pollution and the Death of Man* (1970; Wheaton, IL: Crossway, 2011), 72.

turns out to rank on intelligence scales somewhere between sage hens and bowling balls."[2] This quote was referring to a group of people in the woods deciding which direction to look for the car and then getting lost. But it also applies remarkably well to many environmental policy-makers we see today. Environmental policies are often not formulated by thinkers. They are formulated by forceful personalities who have a knack for saying what itching ears want to hear in order to gain political influence. This is true regarding the environment or anything else. We Christians are too often tossed to and fro by winds of doctrine issuing from leaders in the secular green agenda and reactionaries against them. In this raging war for political influence, it is of utmost importance to anchor ourselves in the Word of God so we can think and act biblically on this very important topic.

So why am I am writing this book? First, mankind was commanded to take godly dominion (Gen. 1:28), and unfortunately secularists have taken up this global responsibility motivated by a number of godless worldviews which have at best produced mixed results. They have been at the helm because Christians have largely abdicated in this area. Second, Christians aren't like-minded and they're supposed to be, particularly on this issue, since the Bible speaks to it so clearly. There is a wide

2. Patrick F. McManus, *A Fine and Pleasant Misery* (New York: Holt, Rinehart, and Winston, 1981), 16.

range of opinions among them on the environment, but very few are carefully thought out and use Scripture as their standard. Often people default to some opinion handed down to them by a very opinionated Christian friend or parent, and that opinion isn't necessarily biblical. Third, there is a huge amount of wonderful biodiversity God created that needs godly dominion. Unfortunately, many Christians are indifferent or apathetic towards nature and biological diversity and have a wrong-headed understanding of the dominion mandate. As a biologist, I have an M.S. in Entomology and a Ph.D. in Environmental Science and Public Policy in which I studied the reproductive ecology of the eastern box turtle. I've done lab research in molecular genetics of bacteria and field research in plant science. In short, I have worked in a variety of subdisciplines in biology and have taught a broad array of biology courses for about 30 years. In addition, as a Christian I have spent a lot of time studying what the Scripture teaches us on this very important matter. I don't want to follow green fads, but neither do I want to fall off the other side of the boat and reject everything that extreme environmentalists hold dear. "The earth is the Lord's and the fullness thereof" (Ps. 24:1, KJV). Environmentalists didn't create the earth or the life on it and they certainly don't own it. I want God's people to reflect on how He views His own creation and how the dominion mandate should be carried out in these modern times where our technological power can be used for great good or great evil towards the living creation. This is a daunting task, but it can be accomplished if we are humble and eager to learn.

I realize it is hard for many to jettison dearly held assumptions, but if we become convinced that they don't line up with Scripture, it is time to give them the boot. I also hope that this book will help you see the living creation through new eyes. Consider the terms "creation" and "the environment." It's funny how the name attached to our surroundings can change how we value it. Our environment is part of the creation, but using the word "environment" makes it sounds like it is the realm and responsibility of secular environmentalists. However, since God made it and we are His heirs, we should be the ones who exercise our authority over it.

As a Christian biologist who is very keen about God's living creation, it's no wonder I've come across a range of opinions (or lack thereof) on environmental issues. So, before I delve into this thorny topic and attempt to lay out a biblically defensible position of how we should view and care for this immense gift from God, I want to first lay out a range of stereotypes held by Christians on the vast topic of the environment. None of these extremes appear to have arisen from careful, thoughtful Bible study. I don't hope to cover every possible view, but you'll get a notion of the broad spectrum of opinions bandied about in Christian circles. This current state of affairs won't do. The universal Church is a far cry away from being like-minded on the environment and every other conceivable topic. Nevertheless, our Lord's command to be like-minded still stands (Phil. 2:2; 1 Pet. 3:8).

CHRISTIAN STEREOTYPES ON THE ENVIRONMENT

1. Anti-green Andy: His position is held primarily in his gut, not in his head. His beliefs are embedded in a deep personal conviction of mankind's dominion over creation, private property rights, and American individualism. He believes that God made us in His image and put us in charge over all creation. Therefore, we are to fill it up with *us*, using or discarding whatever is in our way. We should develop, consume, exploit the earth's resources with little to no concern for cultivating and beautifying them for future generations such that they thrive and become more glorious under our care. Let future generations figure out how to survive in the smoking crater we left them. Anyone who rejects man's dictatorship over creation due to the belief that we are no more important than animals will receive his palpable disdain. He is deathly afraid to be associated with anything an environmentalist may hold dear, so he defaults to a contrarian position on all environmental

concerns. He sees their silly excesses, spin of the data, wrong-headed thinking, and ridiculous heavy-handed governmental regulations, but doesn't want to bother distinguishing baby from bathwater.

2. PreMill Pete: He thinks God only cares about our spiritual state. Getting people saved is all that really matters. He thinks our bodies are necessary to hand out Gospel tracts and our living environment is God's temporary provision to keep our earthly tents propped up while we evangelize during our fleeting tenure on earth. There is no need to concern ourselves with the state of the physical creation because in the end it's all gonna burn with fervent heat (2 Pet. 3:10), probably sooner rather than later. We just need to get people saved before the Rapture. Once we're off this rock we can live forever in our heavenly dwellings.

3. Apathetic April: She hasn't really thought about the environment much. She just exists, eats, sleeps, works, Facebooks, watches movies, and goes to church. She has a vague notion that we are to be good stewards. Heck if she knows what that means . . . recycle?

4. Green Greta: She claims that Christians are supposed to be good stewards. That means uber-green. Everything she eats is 100% organic and gluten-free. GMOs are from the pit of Hell. She recycles every conceivable thing. She's a global warming alarmist

and therefore is guilt-ridden about exhaling CO_2 and driving her car. She attempts to atone for her carbon footprint sins by acquiring eco-indulgences. They include driving a hybrid car, shopping at the co-op, walking to work (when she's not late), and taking quick, lukewarm showers. She also plans to have 1.7 kids. She loves fair trade because it's fair, and it's not nice to be unfair. She voted for Obama because he's green and that's cool. She gets more upset at the death of endangered animals than abortion because endangered animals are rare and people aren't.

There are many other positions that fall between these exaggerated stereotypes. Now, you might be saying to yourself, "Gordon, *you* might be wrong too!" I freely acknowledge that possibility. However, I have spent my career studying these issues as they relate to the Bible and to biology and to the environmental movement at large, so read what I have to say and evaluate my application of Scripture, like the Bereans (Acts 17:11).

In case you still think I'm stereotyping unfairly, let me mention just a few real-life examples. And rest assured that I've met people like this face-to-face. I'm sure you have too.

Anti-green Andy: You couldn't ask for a better Anti-green Andy than Ann Coulter. As she said on live TV, "God gave us the earth. We have dominion over the plants, the animals, the trees. God said, 'Earth is yours. Take it. Rape it. It's yours.'"[3]

The PreMill Pete approach is perfectly summarized by the folks at the Rapture Ready website. "I can only ask where the Bible even hints that saving the whales and fighting global warming are part of the Great Commission. Dealing with environmental problems needs to be left to the politicians . . . If the world is going to be 'dissolved,' there is no need for us to become too attached to it."[4]

It's harder to find published examples of Apathetic April because she hasn't thought about environmental issues long enough to put two words together. But apathy about the environment has reached record highs in the past few years, according to Gallup. You can confirm this by asking your cubicle neighbor how often he thinks about stewarding the environment.[5]

Green Gretas are everywhere as well, because it's the cool (and funded) opinion to have. The very progressive "religion and culture writer" Jonathan Merritt is a perfect example, as he got a book deal out of his opinions:

3. Anne Coulter, guest appearance on *Hannity and Colmes*, June 20, 2001.
4. Todd Strandberg, "Bible Prophecy and Environmentalism," *Rapture Ready*, February 8, 2018, http://www.raptureready.us/rr-environmental.html.
5. Jeffrey M. Jones, "In U.S., Concern About Environmental Threats Eases," Gallup, March 25, 2015, http://news.gallup.com/poll/182105/concern-environmental-threats-eases.aspx?utm_source=Politics&utm_medium=newsfeed&utm_campaign=tiles.

"God is green. The idea seems bizarre, almost trivial. Yet, I'm as sure of that statement as I am that two plus two is four and the mixing of red and yellow makes orange."[6]

I don't want to guilt-trip anyone; I want to encourage each of us to see where we fall on this spectrum and then ask ourselves honestly whether our opinion is formed from a mishmash of opinions handed down from friends or foes, or whether it is a position solidly grounded in Scripture and good science. This requires careful thought and a love for the truth. Ideas that conform to Scripture should be kept and fine-tuned according to the Bible; ideas that don't measure up to Scripture or scientific scrutiny must be discarded regardless of how near and dear they are to us. Much of what scientists say isn't factual at all; often it is their opinions based on highly tenuous assumptions riding on the ethos of their scientific credentials. Being a part of the scientific community for so long, I have developed a knack for seeing a hidden (or not so hidden) agenda and knowing when scientists are really on thin ice. When this is the case, I trust them about as far as I can throw their hybrid car. Proverbs 18:17 says, "The one who states his case first seems right, until the other comes and examines him." There may be environmental policies that seem to be good at face value, but we should do our homework

6. Jonathan Merritt, *Green Like God* (New York: Hachette Book Group, 2010), 1.

before we hitch our wagon to it. Any environmental policies (even decent ones) founded on any cornerstone other than Christ will go awry sooner or later. We must have the mind of Christ, and not just on what we consider spiritual topics. The Scriptures give us a roadmap not just on how we are to live, but how we are to think about everything. This includes the creation. The Scriptures in principle show us how we are to understand our relationship to nature and how we are to exercise dominion over it.

In Part 1 of this book I want to lay out the biblical basis for our rule over the living creation in light of the dominion mandate of Genesis 1:28. Unfortunately there are truncated or distorted interpretations of what the dominion mandate means. I hope to present a robust and distinctive view of biblical dominion, and I will outline biblical reasons for wise dominion as I explain why biological diversity is something we must not ruin or squander. In Part 2, I shift from Bible teacher to Biology teacher and discuss the major practical reasons for wise dominion. In Part 3, I lay out the environmental problems we face today and propose potential biblical solutions.

DISCUSSION QUESTIONS

1. Which stereotype describes you best and why?

2. If you are shown to be in error biblically and ecologically, are you ready to change your view of how dominion should be exercised?

2. THE FOUNDATION FOR CONSERVATION

In dire necessity somebody might write another 'Iliad,' or paint
an 'Angelus,' but fashion a goose? 'I, the Lord, will answer
them. The hand of the Lord hath done this, and the Holy One
of Israel created it.'

ALDO LEOPOLD[7]

IN THIS CHAPTER I WANT TO ESTABLISH
that the dominion mandate, Genesis 1:28, is the foundational command behind conservation, and that the
underlying reason for this imperative is God's own evaluation of His work. As is the case on almost every topic,
the answers start in Genesis. Genesis 1:31 says, "And

7. Aldo Leopold and Charles Walsh Schwartz, *A Sand County Almanac*
(Oxford: OUP, 1968), 229-230.

God saw everything that he had made, and behold, it was very good. And there was evening and there was morning, the sixth day."

We see earlier in chapter 1 that God created the plants (day 3), swimming and flying animals (day 5), beasts of the earth, livestock, creeping things and man (day 6). In verse 31 He clearly states that all life, along with everything else, "was very good." This verse is extremely important because it's foundational to shaping our opinion of all creation. In order for us to have a good and proper assessment of all of life in all of its diversity, we need to know what value God places on His own work. If God painted a picture on a canvas it would be prudent of us to first see what He thinks of it before we go shooting off our mouth about it.

Many Christians are eager to make judgments on God's artwork, as if they know better about what He should or shouldn't have created. I realize that many people aren't keen on a variety of plants and animals for various reasons, e.g. thistles, stinging nettles, poison ivy, yellow jackets, spiders, slugs, snakes, mosquitoes . . . We say they're dangerous, scary, damaging to our property, a health hazard, a nuisance, etc. I grant that many of them are a problem and need to be dealt with as a threat or hazard, but we must keep in mind that many were twisted after the Fall in a variety of ways. His statement, "It was very good," was pronounced *before* He cursed His masterpiece of creation: for example, thorns and thistles, and predator-prey or pathogen-host relationships were a result of His curse on the creation (Gen. 3:18; Rom. 5:12). All plants and animals were perfectly benign in every respect prior to the Fall. I believe that those who were ordained to become predators, parasites, and pathogens (biological natural evil)[8] were genetically front-loaded by God with exquisitely designed weapon systems. When Adam sinned, they actually became predators, parasites, and pathogens. Examples include hypodermic fangs and venom glands of many snakes and stinging cells of cnidarians (jellyfish, sea anemones, etc.). Many insidious parasites and pathogens have complicated life cycles that wreak havoc on their hosts.

Since much of the living creation was twisted after the Fall, how should we view them in light of the dominion mandate? Should we permanently despise and dispose of those creatures that seem to be the most accursed, or should we seek their restoration? While admittedly there are cursed plants and animals that must be kept under control for man to exercise dominion well, this doesn't mean global extermination. Many of our pests wouldn't be pests if they were in the right place and in the right

8. Biological natural evil does not mean willful, culpable rebellion against God. Rather, it means these various weapon systems were created to deal out death and destruction in a post-Fall world. It is a judgment against our sin and a part of the curse.

quantities. Also, some things we consider pests aren't really pests. We may simply have a strange aversion to perfectly harmless plants and animals, due to their inability to conform to our sense of beauty or utility. This can be fixed by a simple attitude adjustment. In other instances, the problem is poor management. Due to our actions (deliberate or accidental) certain species wind up in the wrong place or their population gets out of hand. Their status as pests is because of their ability to negatively affect us in some way or another and to get out from under our control very easily.

Consider this parallel. Christians seek to save the lost through the preaching of the Gospel. We aren't on a crusade to exterminate unbelievers. In the same way, much of creation, including the living part, is bent and distorted to various degrees due to the curse. Romans 8:22 says, "The whole creation has been groaning together in the pains of childbirth until now," but we can with certainty look forward to its future glory: "The creation itself will be set free from its bondage to corruption and obtain the freedom of the glory of the children of God" (Rom. 8:21). We must not be eager to blot out those parts of creation that we deem more accursed. Rather we should work toward their ultimate redemption. We are excited about the redemption of lost souls, but don't seem to understand how wide-sweeping God is in His redemptive plans. Remember, "The creation itself will be set free from its bondage to corruption . . ." Let's think God's lavish and merciful thoughts after Him, rather than in our own stingy categories.

Many secularists are desperately eager to come up with reasons to save this or that species from extinction. Often the value of an endangered or threatened plant or animal is exaggerated. For example, "Sea otters are extremely essential to the kelp forests. If they go extinct the ecosystem will be jeopardized." "American ginseng has many medicinal uses. Without it, many people will suffer." "Some endangered tropical frogs are an attraction for ecotourism. Without them, the industry will decline, along with the emotional wellbeing of nature-lovers." "Many wild animals and plants are essential to certain religious ceremonies. Without them, their religious practices will be hindered." And so on. Even though some of these reasons are valid, the primary reason for conservation should not be anchored in the utility of the species or society's opinion of it. Why? Because no absolute valuation standard can be found there; we are too subject to change. Conservationists are zealous to come up with compelling ecological, aesthetic, utilitarian, or sociological reasons to elevate its value in the eyes of the public. They feel they probably won't get enough buy-in unless they sensationalize the importance of this or that ecosystem or species. I don't dispute that many habitats and species have untold (and undiscovered) value for the welfare of mankind either directly or indirectly. I also think we should continue to explore and unveil the hidden treasures that God's living creation has for us and for the creation as a whole. But if we at present don't happen to have a comprehensive list of ways a particular species is valuable, that doesn't mean it's without value. In such cases, the value of creatures has become too dependent on man's opinion. It's all about getting each species to win a popularity contest. If a particular species' future in some way hinges on whether we give it a thumbs up or thumbs down, conservationists will go on a tireless crusade to persuade the masses to give it a thumbs up. In other words, if a threatened or endangered species needs our help, conservationists must attempt to justify its existence by showing how beneficial it is to humanity in some way or another. This is relatively easy if the species is big, cute, and furry like the giant panda bear. It's a totally different ballgame if the animal in question is a small, boring, brown and gray moth no one even knows exists; or some despised venomous snake, like the Russell's viper, responsible for thousands of deaths each year; or the gray wolf, considered by hunters and ranchers to be a scourge to big game and cattle. These creatures are hard pressed to justify their existence to the general public. Yes, certain biological or conservation societies may value them for ecological, aesthetic, or scientific reasons, but these reasons aren't taken very seriously by the lay community who despise them and don't really grasp their ecological significance. I think snakes are amazing and beautiful, but I can talk till I'm blue in the face to people who hate snakes. My argumentation may be fierce and lucid, but I won't prevail on them a bit. Though I enjoy winning converts to my snake fan club, my opinion isn't what matters. What matters is what God proclaimed after day 6. We might not think this or that creature is particularly useful, particularly pretty, particularly interesting (we might not know it even exists), but we do know it has absolute value simply because God made it and said it was good. Someone might object by saying that after the Fall certain creatures ceased to be good. Regardless, the dominion mandate still stands. Good management and pest control, yes; extermination unto extinction, no. Wise dominion seeks to restrain problematic pests, but the ultimate goal should be to redeem and restore them.

In short, for the Christian, plant and animal species need not justify their existence to us by having some obvious list of humanitarian benefits they can bestow on society. Nor do they need to have some mysterious, ecological trait that enhances some ecosystem in some subtle way (which they probably do). Neither should it require an advocate to ceaselessly champion their rightful place on earth. Their value is intrinsic and divinely granted at creation. It is not dependent on our attitude toward them. Their innate value and written charter for existence are in the words spoken in Genesis, "And God saw everything that he had made, and behold, *it was very good.*"

DISCUSSION QUESTIONS

1. Briefly describe the basis for a species' value.

2. Can we fight pests and still value them? Explain.

3. Can we be avid hunters and conservationists? Explain.

3. FOOD . . . AND OTHER GOOD STUFF

You cause the grass to grow for the livestock
and plants for man to cultivate,
that he may bring forth food from the earth
and wine to gladden the heart of man,
oil to make his face shine
and bread to strengthen man's heart.

PSALM 104:14–15

ANOTHER REASON FOR CONSERVATION OF THE creation is that life was given to us for food (though it is usually dead when we eat it). Without it our "earthly tents," needless to say, would fall down and fall apart. Plants were for our sustenance from the beginning: "Behold, I have given you every plant yielding seed that is on the face of all the earth, and every tree with seed in its fruit. You shall have them for food" (Gen. 1:29). If we believe the secular story, then plants were evolving purposelessly and fruit was never intended by God for human and animal nutrition or medicine. It was just a happy evolutionary coincidence that they evolved nutritious reproductive structures that taste good to animals and to us and that happen to have useful pharmaceuticals tucked away in their tissues. Although evolutionists would avoid the word "purpose," they would grant that there are evolutionary reasons for the interdependency of life. For example, attractive flowers were naturally selected because attracting pollinators was advantageous, because flowers need to be pollinated to reproduce successfully. Tasty, fleshy fruits were also naturally selected, because ingested fruit is one way to disperse seeds from the parents and plant them in ready-made fertilizer. We need not object to the functionality of pretty flowers or tasty fruits. Yes, they are selectively advantageous, but their beauty and taste was no evolutionary accident. They were made and designed by a loving God not only for their own reproduction, but also for nutrition and the enjoyment of man and animals.

ANIMALS FOR FOOD AND MUCH MORE

In Genesis 9:3, God opens up the menu to include animals: "Every moving thing that lives shall be food for you." Animal flesh was also intended to provide sustenance for us after the Flood. In the Old Covenant, both plants and animals are used for sacrifices. The Lord made the first garments from animal hides to clothe Adam and Eve's nakedness. Leather, hair, and wool are mentioned many times in the Scripture in making various articles of clothing. The phrase "a land flowing with milk and honey" clearly expresses the manifold blessing of God to the children of Israel.

Life is interdependent. Milk and honey do not arise from nothing. Milk for human consumption is mostly produced by cattle and goats. These two animals, of course, need good pasture. Good pasture needs fertile soil and rain. Bees need nectar-producing flowers. All of this is from the hand of God.

It is easy to fall into a perfunctory mindset when we thank God in the abstract for our food, clothing, and homes. Perfunctory prayers occur when we don't see God, His creation, and the human secondary causes He has ordained to cultivate, harvest, and bring these blessings to us, i.e. farmers, ranchers, loggers, carpenters, clothing manufacturers, employees in the produce or meat section of the grocery store, chefs, cooks, etc. We thank God in the abstract by not pondering Him as the source of the blessings or the source of the means He uses to bring all of this to us. Without Him we would have none of it. Ponder that for a moment. Think of the chain of events that produced the food and brought the food to you and thank God. He created the animals and plants that provide us

our food and so much more, but He also sovereignly or-
chestrates every step along the long and convoluted way to
our mouths, clothing, and homes.

Many things today might not be safe to eat, but there
are probably many more plants and animals that could be
enlisted for our gastronomic pleasures and other needs. I
am in awe of how much more variety has appeared in the
grocery stores in the last several decades of my existence.
Part of this variety is due to globalization, and I'm sure
people in the food industry will continue to explore new
ways to combine what we already have into new dishes
as they keep exploring the riches of creation to expand
the already immense global menu. When people like the
taste of something, a demand for it arises, and supply
attempts to meet that demand. Consequently, we can
and have overharvested nature for particular plants or
animals, seriously depleting their populations, even to
the point of driving them to extinction. Overfishing and
bycatch are just two examples that are of serious concern
in the global fishing industry. We have done this in the
past, and we are beginning to learn from our mistakes.[9]
Many nations are becoming increasingly aware of the
concept of sustainability and are seeking to implement it
in food production through the farming and husbandry

9. Jonathan Wood, "Is the Era of Overfishing Coming to a Close in the
U.S.?" *Property and Environmental Research Center,* June 11, 2018,
https://www.perc.org/2018/06/11/is-the-era-of-overfishing-coming-to
-a-close-in-the-u-s/.

of plants and animals that we like or need. Happily, this takes the pressure off the wild populations that can be depleted, extirpated, or driven to extinction.

You might be wondering why I am bringing all this up. Of course we eat fruit and wear leather and have homes made of wood! Of course a lot of pharmaceuticals are plant derived! Why make a point of it if it is so obvious? My point is to show from Scripture that our use of these things is part of God's purpose. It is true that humans are clever. They figured out how to use plant and animal products in countless ways—but God made those living resources and made us clever. This is important to point out, because we quickly start taking these blessings for granted. Also, when tens of millions of people like something *a lot*, there is a big demand for it, and certain people try to meet that demand by cultivating it or harvesting it from the wild. If the latter occurs, then overharvesting can threaten or endanger the plant or animal. We need reminders that when we eat plants, use plant-derived pharmaceuticals as medicine, eat bacon or burgers, wear leather boots and belts, enjoy our cotton and linen clothing, and relax in the coziness of our homes, God intended all of those uses from the very beginning. Acknowledging this adds heartfelt gratitude to our prayers of thanksgiving and makes us more circumspect about how our consumption affects the supply of these God-given blessings. Remember that greed for stuff or money can easily lead to overharvest or wanton slaughter of these living resources. Prudent and thankful consumption will be blessed.

DISCUSSION QUESTIONS

1. List five ways plants were used in the Bible other than food.

2. List five ways animals were used in the Bible other than food.

3. What should be our response to these manifold uses? How can we nurture this response?

4. THE DOMINION MANDATE: HE COMMANDED US TO CARE FOR IT

Be fruitful and multiply and fill the earth and subdue it,

and have dominion over the fish of the sea

and over the birds of the heavens

and over every living thing that moves on the earth.

GENESIS 1:28

IN PSALM 8, WHEN HE CONSIDERS THE majesty of God and the lowliness of man, King David is amazed that God would even think about us, let alone put us in charge of all animal life.

When I look at your heavens, the work of your fingers,

the moon and the stars, which you have set in place,

what is man that you are mindful of him,

and the son of man that you care for him?

29

> Yet you have made him a little lower than the heavenly
> > beings
> > and crowned him with glory and honor.
> You have given him dominion over the works of your
> > hands;
> > you have put all things under his feet,
> all sheep and oxen,
> > and also the beasts of the field,
> the birds of the heavens, and the fish of the sea,
> > whatever passes along the paths of the seas.
> O LORD, our Lord,
> > how majestic is your name in all the earth! (vv. 3–9)

God putting us in charge and telling us to rule over fish, birds, and every land animal is what theologians call the dominion mandate. As we look over world history there are countless examples of humans using living things in lawful ways as previously mentioned (food, clothing, medicine, housing, shipping, furniture, etc.). Unfortunately, there are also many examples where our unrestrained greed or stupidity has led to overharvest of timber or the deliberate slaughter of many species of animals, leading them to the brink of extinction, or even to complete extinction.[10] Our massive efforts to propagate a few plants to feed, clothe, and house ourselves have led us to hold a truncated

10. Look under "Restoration" in chapter 10 for examples.

view of God's manifold botanical blessings and to a lack of appreciation for the immense diversity of plants God has created. Plants, in all their overwhelming variety can offer us so much more than food, clothing, and shelter. They can enrich our lives in many other tangible and intangible ways.

So, what is dominion? The Hebrew word for "to have dominion," *radah*, is lexically a strong word.[11] It is the royal rule of a king. The Merriam-Webster definitions that approximate it are "supreme authority," "sovereignty," "absolute ownership."[12] This is weightier than stewardship because it includes ownership. But how do we exercise this authority and ownership in light of all Scripture? Taken wrongly, this definition can seem to give mankind a blank check to do as we please without dealing with consequences. Supreme authority and absolute ownership do not mean there is no accountability or no consequences for our actions. We can own a car but still get a speeding ticket, ruin the engine by not changing the oil, or wrap it around a tree trunk by driving drunk. God made the world in such a way that we reap what we sow. Nevertheless, God signed the title of

---

11. Strong's concordance defines it as "to rule, have dominion, dominate, tread down" (Blue Letter Bible.org, s.v. "Raddah," H7287, https://www.blueletterbible.org/lang/Lexicon/Lexicon.cfm?strongs=H7287&t=KJV).

12. *Merriam-Webster*, s.v. "dominion (n.)," https://www.merriam-webster.com/dictionary/dominion, definitions 2 and 5.

the living creation over to us in Genesis 1:26–30. It is up to us to exercise dominion wisely, not foolishly.

As with all gifts granted to us by God, they can be unappreciated, mismanaged, squandered, and ruined. God gave us creation to exercise dominion over it, and through the millennia our track record has not been good. This is because, as individuals, societies, and nations, we have not endeavored to rule over it as He rules over us. We have extinguished many species and ruined many glorious ecosystems due to our greed, stupidity, or apathy. As Christians, we need to begin imitating God's character if we are to exercise godly dominion. What does godly dominion look like? To illustrate, let's look at a smaller yet very important institution: marriage. Paul describes how we are to view this institution in Ephesians 5:23–27:

> For the husband is the head of the wife even as Christ is the head of the church, his body, and is himself its Savior. Now as the church submits to Christ, so also wives should submit in everything to their husbands. Husbands, love your wives, as Christ loved the church and gave himself up for her, that he might sanctify her, having cleansed her by the washing of water with the word, so that he might present the church to himself in splendor, without spot or wrinkle or any such thing, that she might be holy and without blemish.

In this familiar passage we see that the husband is the head of the wife. This makes many Christians who have drunk the Kool-Aid of today's egalitarianism cringe. But what if we simply have a messed-up view of headship? We can breathe easier when we see that headship in marriage is actually a picture of Christ and the Church. This tells us an awful lot about godly dominion, and we should flush our false view of dominion down the drain. Look at the main imperative: Love your wives. How? As Christ loved the Church. What kind of love is it? Sacrificial love. Christ gave Himself up for her. Why? To sanctify her, cleanse her, wash her. To what end? To present the Church to Himself in splendor, without spot or wrinkle or any such thing, so that she might be holy and without blemish. Christ is the head of the Church with the same robust definition of dominion I gave earlier.

Look at how wonderful dominion can be when it is done according to the pattern God gave us. Christ-like dominion rules through loving sacrifice, not tyranny. Too many Christians have conflated dominion with oppressive rule: "Let's see how much we can exploit those we rule over with brute force." But Christian dominion is servant-like, giving and not exploitive. It cleanses and washes and beautifies. A husband that exercises this kind of headship makes his wife thrive and flourish and become more fruitful. Through his sacrificial love and leadership, she also grows more radiant and beautiful. Our dominion over creation should follow a similar pattern because that is God's character. Biblical dominion over creation should have lovely results if we follow the same pattern. We are to exercise dominion over the living world, whether it's just our pets, our backyard, our garden, our farm and livestock, whether it's our city parks or national parks, so that whatever is entrusted to our care can thrive, and never languish or be ruined or squandered. It should be made more beautiful and flourish, just like a cherished wife. I'm not advocating veganism or vegetarianism due to a sentimentalized view of animals where hunting game or slaughtering livestock is frowned upon. Not at all; it is lawful to eat meat and supply that demand as a rancher or an avid hunter. The point is to exercise dominion in such a way that what belongs to us is cared for. God blesses obedience. Jacob's flocks thrived and increased because of God's blessing, but at the same time God uses means. Jacob slaughtered and ate from his flocks, but he also knew and cared for their needs. He led them to good pasture and watered them. He bred them to be stronger. He did not drive them too hard. Like Jacob, we should be responsible, diligent husbandmen. This involves being a student of what we own, whether it is a pet snake, dog, cat, thousands of cattle, or huge tracts of wilderness. We have to know our charges well so that we can adequately care for them. The bigger the charge, the more we have to know. The responsibility can be immense.

Today the common buzzword dealing with natural resources is sustainability. Compared with diminishing our natural resources or causing extinction or extirpation (deliberately or inadvertently), sustainability is a big step in the right direction. However, it isn't good enough. Consider the parable of the talents in Matthew 25. Which servant got chewed out by the master? The servant that was just thinking about sustainability. He took his talent and buried it in the ground. When the master returned, he delivered to him exactly what he was given and got in trouble for it, because he didn't invest it (Matt. 25:24–30). The faithful servants managed to get a net return. They turned a profit and were given praise and a reward. When we apply this lesson to the dominion mandate (that is, wildlife management at a global scale), which of the following seems most consistent with God's character? 1) Manage the created diversity such that "useless" plants and animals can be *diminished* to make room for "useful" plants and animals; 2) manage the created diversity such that they are all merely *sustained*; or 3) manage the created diversity such that "useful" plants and animals *thrive* under domestication or are well managed in the wild and "useless" plants and animals *thrive* in the wild or in captivity. Number 3 is the most consistent with the character of God and His

Gospel. Truth, beauty, and goodness should be coupled to the dominion mandate in a very deliberate and purposeful way.

DISCUSSION QUESTIONS

1. Name two ways we've exercised dominion wrongly.

2. Why should we move past the notion of sustainability?

3. Why is Christ's headship over the Church a good pattern for us to follow in our exercise of the dominion mandate?

5. MAINTAINING THE CREATED DIVERSITY

A land ethic of course cannot prevent the alteration, manage-
ment, and use of these 'resources,' but it does affirm their right
to continued existence, and, at least in spots, their continued
existence in their natural state.

ALDO LEOPOLD[13]

A PERSON, A COMPANY, OR A NATION
could possibly take very good care of those plants and animals that they highly value. Most people that love and own
horses or dogs or roses take good care of them, particularly
if it is their livelihood. In the same way, some nations make
a valiant effort to take good care of a national wildlife icon.
For example, China is well known as the home of the giant panda bear, and they labor hard to maintain a good

13. Leopold and Schwartz, 240.

natural habitat and breed captive animals. Whether it's at the individual level or national level, poor dominion can result in shame or financial loss or both, not to mention extinction. So even though the exercise of dominion may be admirable when applied to certain plants or animals, that may not mean that it's extended to all plants and animals. And that needs to be remedied.

There are two main reasons laid out in Scripture that give us clear direction regarding the conservation of all plants and animals. As already mentioned, the first reason to maintain the created diversity is God's five-star evaluation of His own masterpiece—the creation (which of course includes the enormous variety of plants and animals on this planet). In Genesis 1:31, God says after creating everything, "It is very good." Therefore, what God says is *very good* is worth conserving. But conserving is not enough. Since the God of the universe said it was *very good*, it's worth cherishing. Recall they don't need to justify their existence by being of practical use to us. God made them, said they were good, and that's the only endorsement they need in order to be valued by us. The relative abundance of certain plants and animals are definitely affected by personal differences in our utilitarian needs and values. In the chapter "November" in *A Sand County Almanac*, Aldo Leopold writes of his and other biases for and against different trees when it comes to the ax. Here is an excerpt.

> The wielder of an ax has as many biases as there are
> species of trees on his farm. In the course of the years
> he imputes to each species, from his responses to their
> beauty or utility, and their responses to his labors for
> or against them, a series of attributes that constitute a
> character. I am amazed to learn what diverse characters
> different men impute to one and the same tree.[14]

Having different preferences for plants and animals
you choose to have on your property isn't something
to feel guilty about. Cattle and sheep will always outnumber bison and bighorn sheep. Corn and wheat will
outnumber the showy lady's slipper orchid and white
trillium. However, just because we may favor useful or
beautiful plants and animals does not mean that plants
and animals we currently deem useless or unattractive
can be forgotten and accidentally thrown under the bus.

There is one complicating factor that I will briefly
address. Current creationists believe that species diversity has increased since the Creation. Since it is believed that God created *kinds* that had the potential to
diversify into a number of different species, one might
argue that it is not necessary to protect all the diversity
that has resulted since the initial creation. For example,
many creationists believe that the dog family (which
includes coyotes, foxes, jackals, dogs, and wolves) is

14. Leopold and Schwartz, 75.

one created kind. Given this assumption, one might argue that most of these species could go extinct and we're not diminishing the number of created kinds. Provided that we conserve at least one representative species from each kind, it's okay, right? Wrong! There are many, many good ecological (and other) reasons to maintain the current diversity of this family. The many different wild dog species serve many important roles to a variety of ecosystems from the Arctic to the equator. This is true for many other supposed *kinds* as well. Also, there isn't an agreement on what constitutes a *kind*. Secondly, even if we did know the boundaries of each kind, the removal of the genetic breadth is still a detriment to that particular kind. This breadth is like a range of different color paints on a palette of a master painter. If you remove all the colors but one, you sorely limit the artist's options.

Let's get back to biblical reasons. The first reason that we should maintain the created diversity is the simple fact that God created them and said that they are *very good*. This should be a strong reminder that they have a rightful place on earth. We should show concern and care to those underdog species even if they don't commend themselves to us from a utilitarian point of view. Since we love God, it makes perfect sense that we care for all our fellow creatures that He made, even if they appear "useless" to us.

The second reason is God's clear desire to conserve His created diversity during the Flood. In Genesis 7:1–3, we are told why the ark is supposed to be so huge:

> Then the LORD said to Noah, "Go into the ark, you and all your household, for I have seen that you are righteous before me in this generation. Take with you seven pairs of all clean animals, the male and his mate, and a pair of the animals that are not clean, the male and his mate, and seven pairs of the birds of the heavens also, male and female, *to keep their offspring alive on the face of all the earth.*" (emphasis mine)

This is an extraordinary juxtaposition of two very different objectives carried out in the building of the ark and the great Flood. The objective of the Flood was to destroy all terrestrial animal life and mankind off the face of the earth because of mankind's exceedingly great wickedness. The objective of the ark was to preserve a remnant of all terrestrial animal life and mankind during the great Flood. Noah and his family were spared to preserve mankind and pairs of every kind of animal (seven of clean animals) to *keep their offspring alive upon the earth.* In other words, the Flood was the biggest act of judgment on mankind in the history of the world. Noah's Ark, on the other hand, was the biggest act of biodiversity conservation in the history of the world. And both acts were from God. The Flood was a direct act of God. The building of the ark was commanded by God.

If God was only concerned about the animals that were of direct human benefit, then the ark could have been a tiny fraction of the size. Think of all the animal kinds that are directly useful to man—sheep, cattle, goats, chickens, horses, pigs, etc. It doesn't take much room to fit animals that Noah would have considered necessary to build a civilization. It is also worth considering that as man advanced in agriculture, transportation, and medicine since the Flood, other animals were added to the ranks considered helpful to man. Noah probably wouldn't have anticipated the use of mice and rats in biomedical research, yet they have been very helpful in advancing our medical knowledge, not to mention providing food items for unconventional pets.

So just because we don't currently see the benefit of a certain animal or plant doesn't mean someone won't discover it later on. Also, benefit to mankind doesn't necessarily mean a practical use like food, clothing, transportation, and medicine. Some animals just pique our curiosity, others satisfy our desire to see beauty, and others simply fascinate us. This is why almost everyone likes to go to the zoo. Others satisfy our need for companionship (conventional pets like dogs, cats, birds, and hamsters, or unconventional pets like amphibians and reptiles). The list keeps growing.

Some might argue that we should only be putting all our efforts into evangelism and discipleship rather than solving environmental problems. I will discuss this in detail near the end of the book. However, for now I will note that this thinking presupposes that these two goals are at odds. This wrong-headed thinking ignores the fact that Christians can please God in any lawful calling. This great liberating truth was reestablished during the Reformation. To maintain the contrary is no different than saying that Christians should only be pastors and evangelists. This is bad theology. God gave us the world and all that is in it so that we would maintain, utilize, and cause it to flourish under our dominion. To accomplish this requires a whole host of people working as unto the Lord in many lawful callings, including environmental callings.

I also would like to add that many unbelievers have a love for creation. Their love is idolatrous because they deny their Creator. Nevertheless, they still see and enjoy the beauty of creation. I find it an ironic tragedy when non-Christians have a deeper appreciation for the creation than Christians who worship and serve the God who created it. These non-Christians may be more drawn to the Gospel when they see God's people more richly enjoying the creation than they do because they love and serve their Creator.

DISCUSSION QUESTIONS

1. What are the two main biblical reasons to maintain the biodiversity on earth?

2. Assuming that a number of species arose from each created kind, is it more prudent to conserve species diversity within each kind or conserve at least one species from each kind? Explain your answer.

6. A CHRISTIAN VIEW OF ANIMAL CARE

Whoever is righteous has regard for the life of his beast,
but the mercy of the wicked is cruel.

PROVERBS 12:10

GIVEN THE ABOVE VERSE, IT SHOULD
not be a surprise that, relatively speaking, countries whose
people have had a long history of a Christian worldview
treat animals in a God-honoring way. Christian culture
affects both true believers and unbelievers. The former
treat animals better through the transforming power
of the Gospel; the latter treat them better through the
enculturating effect of living in a society that is saturat-
ed with Christian ethics. Apart from the direct application of Scripture and the renewing work of the Holy
Spirit, the theologian who has most greatly influenced

Christian thought on this topic up to the present is Thomas Aquinas. In his *Summa Theologiae*, he argues that cruelty to animals is simply wrong, in part because cruel behavior toward animals can spill over into how we treat our fellow man.[15]

Despite the mainstream Christian teaching against cruelty to animals, not all who call themselves Christians always treat animals well. One horrid example was the Black Stocking Calvinists in Holland who would be cruel to their animals because they assumed they didn't have a soul.[16] Conversely not all non-Christians treat animals poorly. You could easily find exceptions where Christians don't care for or abuse animals and where non-Christians are exemplary in their treatment of animals. Individuals can and often do behave inconsistently with their worldview; however, societies, cultures, and nations usually behave consistently with the prevailing worldview. Countries that are either pre-Christian or post-Christian often show tremendous imbalances or extremes in their treatment of animals. Some show little or no concern for animal welfare or they show too much concern for animal welfare. The latter manifests itself in false religions like Hinduism or Jainism where belief in reincarnation precludes a view of animals as food. People can be starving to death and yet thousands of cattle are untouched because they are revered

15. *Summa Theologiae* II, I, Q102.
16. Schaeffer and Middelmann, *Pollution and the Death of Man*, 42.

as sacred. In a more secular context, animal rights activists have either demoted humans or promoted animals to the point that they would want us to have no more rights than animals do. Since their Darwinian worldview assumes that we are just another animal alongside all other animals, there is no reason to conclude that we should have more rights than them. If we are all just a product of random evolution, then to speak of rights is nonsense. Evolution doesn't produce ethical codes or rights which we are obligated to honor, so this righteous indignation against humans exalting their rights over animal rights is silly. On the other extreme, when a culture views dominion in an exploitive way (use of animals with little regard to their health or welfare in order to make money or make life easier) animals and habitats can be sorely abused. Without an absolute ethical standard derived from a Christian worldview to keep these extremes from happening, animals can be either undervalued or overvalued. It should be noted here that a great hero of the Christian faith, William Wilberforce, who is best known for his valiant efforts to abolish the slave trade, also helped found the first organization for animal welfare—the Society for the Prevention of Cruelty to Animals (the SPCA). All of these efforts were motivated by his Christian faith.

Countries with a strong Christian heritage or foundation are by no means perfect with regard to captive or wild animal treatment. Sin and inconsistencies in

Christian teaching are everywhere. Many atrocious acts of cruelty toward captive animals, wanton slaughter of wild animals, and a complete disregard for the environment while developing the land, have been done due to apathy, antagonism toward wilderness, greed, and an unbiblical understanding of dominion. Regardless of our past track record in the animal care department, when a thoroughgoing Christian worldview saturates a culture, a healthy relationship with animals will take root.

A Christian worldview sees animals as fellow creatures made by God from the dust of the earth. God used the same ingredients to make man and animals. He also made animals before man: Sea and flying creatures on day five and land animals on day six, before Adam. Animals also have the same breath and have spirit (Eccl. 3:19–21). Even though we are made in the image of God and were given dominion, these facts should keep us from becoming too big for our britches. Christians who own animals and who know and seek to obey the Word of God practice husbandry in an honorable way for the reasons mentioned above. If these truths are in your heart and mind, good husbandry is a natural outgrowth. Nevertheless, godly dominion as defined by Scripture gives man sovereign authority over the animals. That means it is lawful to domesticate and breed animals for food, pets, hide, scientific research, and according to the whims of hobbyists. But in so doing, we should treat them with a goodly measure of care and kindness. When animals are killed for food, science, or other products, we must do so using quick and humane methods. Putting animals through unnecessary agony is simply cruel. When animals look to us for food and water, it is our duty to meet their needs in a healthy, timely way. Many of the patriarchs in the Old Testament were shepherds, and we can glean many lessons from them in how they cared for their flocks. Proverbs 27:23–24 says, "Know well the condition of your flocks, and give attention to your herds, for riches do not last forever; and does a crown endure to all generations?" Solomon is teaching us that riches and wealth are not automatic, nor are they a divine right. God made the world in such a way that when we mismanage our property, our livelihood can go up in smoke. People back then were much more tied to the land than we are today, so the truths of biblical husbandry made more sense to them experientially. Nevertheless, whether we grow our own food or not, we still must look to God to provide us with our daily needs for food and clothing. Similarly, since we are like gods to our animals, we should care for them as our Father cares for us.

DISCUSSION QUESTIONS

1. What are a couple of biblical texts that demonstrate that cruelty and abuse to animals is incompatible with Christian behavior?

2. What are the two imbalances in animal treatment that can arise if not grounded in biblical principles? Pick one and give their justification for that treatment.

7. CREATION'S DECLARATION OF GOD'S CARE, GLORY, AND WISDOM

O LORD, how manifold are your works!

In wisdom have you made them all;

the earth is full of your creatures.

PSALM 104:24

IT IS MANIFESTLY CLEAR FROM SCRIPTURE that nature declares the glory and wisdom of God. It is also clear that God doesn't just create man and animals to say, "You're totally on your own." He cares for man and wild beasts. In Psalm 104, it is glorious to read of God's bountiful provision of water, food, and habitat for man and beast. It is not just presented as a cold, hard fact. In Psalm 104:24 quoted above, King David (a man with plenty of experience tending his flocks in the

wilderness) is overflowing with praise and adoration to
God because of His manifold works.

It is clear that David has a deep appreciation, not
just for domesticated animals, but also for the beauty
and glory of wild animals in their natural habitat. His
gratitude and praise to God for creating and sustaining
it all is a wonderful example for us. You should read all
of Psalm 104, but here I just want to point out those
particulars dealing with living things that remind us
who the Creator and Sustainer of life is. As moderns,
it is easy to lapse into the mindset that the world is a
huge network of physical cause/effect relationships. As
Christians we may acknowledge that God is in control,
but too often we think this is only true in some abstract
theological sense. But no, He is the source of all water
to quench the thirst of all the beasts (vv. 10, 11, and 13)
and trees (v. 16). And with those trees He provides birds
with good places to nest and sing (vv. 12 and 17). He
feeds and provides habitat for the wild beasts too (vv. 18,
21, 22, and 25–28) and it is His Spirit that creates them
all (v. 30). God provides grass for the cattle and crops for
us to cultivate (v. 14). Also, He is the source of wine and
bread to gladden and sustain our hearts and oil to make
our faces shine (v. 15). It's also important to consider
that God doesn't obligate Himself to sustain all things.
When He takes away their breath (and He does), they
die and return to dust (v. 29).

Psalm 147:8–9 also says the same thing regarding the source of rain and food for wild animals, particularly lions and ravens.

> He covers the heavens with clouds;
>> he prepares rain for the earth;
>> he makes grass grow on the hills.
> He gives to the beasts their food,
>> and to the young ravens that cry.

Job 38:39–41 reinforces this thought:

> Can you hunt the prey for the lion,
>> or satisfy the appetite of the young lions,
> when they crouch in their dens
>> or lie in wait in their thicket?
> Who provides for the raven its prey,
>> when its young ones cry to God for help,
>> and wander about for lack of food?

Psalm 29:9 tells us that God's word causes deer to bear young: "The voice of the Lord makes the deer give birth." And we see in Job 39:26–30 that God's wisdom created the hawk to soar and the eagle to take flight, build its nest, and spot prey from afar.

> Is it by your understanding that the hawk soars
>> and spreads his wings toward the south?

Is it at your command that the eagle mounts up
and makes his nest on high?
On the rock he dwells and makes his home,
on the rocky crag and stronghold.
From there he spies out the prey;
his eyes behold it from far away.
His young ones suck up blood,
and where the slain are, there is he.

Consider the last few chapters in Job (chapters 38–41). Read it all and consider how animals declare God's glory and how God is sovereign over them all. In answer to all of Job's complaints, God does not respond with some philosophical justification for allowing Satan to afflict Job with intense, prolonged, and excruciating emotional and physical hardship, pain, and disease. Instead He simply gives Job a powerful natural history lesson including who created, controls, and sustains the earth, the sea, the water cycle, the heavens, and the animals. He also reminds Job of his inability to control the constellations and his lack of knowledge and control of the wild donkey, the wild ox, the ostrich, the horse, the hawk, the eagle, and the mountain goats (including their gestational periods). His grand finale is in chapters 40 and 41 where He showcases a couple of His most awesome and mighty creatures—Behemoth and Leviathan. Why does God do this? He is showing Job in no uncertain terms that He is Almighty God, the Creator, Controller, and Sustainer of all things, and that is the ultimate reason why He can allow bad things to happen to good people.

The more we study God's creation, the more overwhelmed we become with His majesty, power, wisdom, and intelligence. An artist that studies, teaches, and imitates great art becomes a better artist. An engineer that studies, teaches, and imitates great engineering becomes a better engineer. The same is true for cooking, sculpting, and writing; I suppose it is true for any skill. So how do we become wiser? I Kings 4:33–34 describes King Solomon's wisdom:

> He spoke of trees, from the cedar that is in Lebanon to the hyssop that grows out of the wall. He spoke also of beasts, and of birds, and of reptiles, and of fish. And people of all nations came to hear the *wisdom* of Solomon, and from all the kings of the earth, who had heard of his wisdom. (emphasis added)

What is curious about this passage is that wisdom is not just the ability to make correct moral judgments given a complicated situation. It also includes a knowledge of natural history. We may think that Solomon's plant and animal teachings were nothing more than moral lessons that we can glean from simple facts about plants and animals. For example, "Go to the ant, O sluggard;

consider her ways, and be wise" (Prov. 6:6). Ants are obviously industrious and lazy people can learn a thing or two about hard work by looking at ants. But it's much more than that. There is no reason to think that Solomon wasn't teaching basic truths about animal and plant biology, and this was considered part of Solomon's wisdom. In light of the fact that God's wisdom is revealed in creation in the same way that an engineer's wisdom is revealed in his engineering, then to study it should make one wiser.

> Great are the works of the LORD,
>> studied by all who delight in them.
> (Ps. 111:2)

DISCUSSION QUESTIONS

1. In what ways does God provide for His creatures? Give several passages that describe His provision.

2. What creatures does God use to display His glory and wisdom? What features are highlighted in each?

3. Can we gain wisdom through the study of His creatures? Explain.

PART 2: PRACTICAL REASONS FOR WISE DOMINION

8. CREATION: OUR LIFE SUPPORT SYSTEM

Water, soil, and the earth's green mantle of plants
make up the world that supports the animal life of the earth.

RACHEL CARSON[17]

IN PART 1, I LAID OUT BIBLICAL REA-
sons for wise dominion over all life: first, God said it
was *very good*, and that evaluation sets the foundation
for how we are to value life on earth; second, He gave us
living things to feed, shelter, cure, and clothe us; third,
He commanded us as image-bearers to take dominion
over all life on earth; fourth, He shows that He wants us
to maintain the diversity by His command to Noah to
build a huge ark to accommodate all terrestrial creatures;

17. *The Silent Spring: The Classic that Launched the Environmental Movement*
(New York: Houghton Mifflin, 2002), 63.

fifth, He teaches us in Scripture that we are to care for our fellow creatures; and lastly, creatures, whether wild or domesticated, declare God's care, glory, and wisdom. If we exercise poor dominion, it doesn't showcase God's artwork as well. Wise dominion does.

In Part 2 I will present practical reasons for wise dominion. Some will overlap with the reasons in Part 1, some are quite obvious, and still others have only been unveiled through a lot of scientific research.

Creation is our life support system. Plants and fungi were the only thing on the menu at first (Gen. 1:29), and then after Noah's Flood, God expanded the menu to include animals (Gen. 9:3). Needless to say, without plants and animals we would all die.

Even many secular people innately know that we have dominion (in their view due to our highly evolved brain) and act accordingly. Certain people in the food business are searching for new foods or new ways to combine them to create new dishes. This should be done lawfully and with reasons that glorify God. Christians with a culinary calling should join this pursuit with greater motivation than their secular comrades who think we are nothing more than naked apes with inflated brains. We should have greater motivation because we also have a clear command from God to fill the earth and subdue it. This should include something beyond a subsistence mentality. Dominion in providing food should include the pursuit of truth, beauty, and goodness. In this pursuit we can look at life on earth (plants and animals) as a grand, global pantry from which to select ingredients. Nevertheless, we must be ecologically circumspect by having a deep commitment to maintaining a healthy supply of these living ingredients. If we look at a restaurant's pantry, we would consider the chef unwise and shortsighted if he allowed certain ingredients to run low or run out. We may know how to keep our personal shelves stocked, but we must keep in mind that the ultimate source of all food is the wild. Even though most ingredients have been cultivated or domesticated for thousands of years, we must wisely maintain this diversity of wild plants and animals, not only because it was very good, but also as a reservoir of new food items. It is from the wild that we originally stocked our pantries. And it is from there that we will continue to add to them.

Food is of obvious practical value, and we must not take it for granted. Overflowing gratitude to God is the proper foundation in the pursuit of food, but that same gratitude should provide checks and balances in that pursuit. If we forget that all these blessings are from God's hand, we may show little restraint in our consumption. If it promises to be a quick source of wealth, and greed is left unchecked, it snowballs into wanton slaughter, which can easily result in extinction. We may camouflage our greed by calling it healthy ambition or an entrepreneurial spirit, but we can tell whether we are actually doing the right thing if we ask ourselves whether we are thinking generationally and covenantally. We need to love our neighbor now, but we also need to love our future descendants. Proverbs 13:22 says, "A good man leaves an inheritance to his children's children, but the sinner's wealth is laid up for the righteous." We shouldn't just think about inheritance as money and property for our immediate family. We also need to think about passing on the inheritance of the created biodiversity at the global scale. Plants and animals were bequeathed by God to Adam and Eve (and to us through them), and it's paramount that we exercise wise dominion such that we pass on that same global inheritance to our descendants. Wise dominion doesn't just sustain the inheritance: it increases it.

But that isn't the only thing we need to exercise godly dominion over. If food is essential and can be taken for granted, let's consider something that is just as essential to life but is less tangible. Oxygen gas (invisible, tasteless, and odorless) is just that. It comprises about 21% of the earth's atmosphere. Mankind and virtually all animal and plant life require it for cellular respiration. To metabolize our food, oxygen must be inhaled, enter our bloodstream, and be delivered to every living cell in our body so that we can literally burn our fuel (food) to generate the energy we need to live productive lives. Where does most of our oxygen come from? It comes from the magical process called photosynthesis, carried out in the leaves and stems of plants. But photosynthesis isn't just carried out by land plants. About half of all photosynthetic oxygen production is accomplished by algae and photosynthetic bacteria in the world's watery environments (mostly oceans, but also streams, rivers, ponds, swamps, lakes, and estuaries). Even if we don't eat these unsung heroes, they keep us all breathing easy. Not only do they keep us chugging away with the oxygen, they also keep almost all machinery chugging away. Whether it be engines for transportation or generators in power plants, any machine that runs on combustion of fuel requires that precious gas called oxygen. Even much of our electricity is supplied by the oxygen-requiring combustion in power plants. Therefore, it behooves us to take good care of this diverse army of plants and algae that keep us constantly supplied with this essential yet invisible gas.

There is yet another practical reason to preserve all this wonderful biodiversity. I would be remiss if I didn't mention the fact that plants, fungi, and animals (especially plants and fungi) are the original source of many pharmaceuticals. God has hidden away many chemicals in the tissues of plants and animals that have many medicinal uses. Proverbs 25:2 says, "It is the glory of God to conceal things, but the glory of kings is to search things out." God did not inform us of all the possible practical uses of plants and animals. Instead He made us in His image and gave us big, clever, curious, problem-solving brains, and then told us to figure things out and solve problems.

One of the ways we do this is by looking to nature for cures to our diseases and other biomedical uses. In the sciences we have again and again found chemicals that can kill or control dangerous microbes that have gained access into our bodies. Alexander Fleming in 1928 made an accidental, yet revolutionary discovery. He found a mold contaminant on one of his Petri dishes that had some bacteria growing on it. Fleming noticed that there was a clear halo around the mold colony. He deduced that it was due to the presence of some mysterious chemical the fungus was producing which inhibited bacterial growth. As a result, he discovered the first antibiotic, and the chemical was named Penicillin, after the genus of the contaminating mold *Penicillium*. Though it took a decade or so to figure out how to mass produce it, it was just in time for World War II and saved countless lives.

Another fungal-derived compound was cyclosporine, which is widely used as an immunosuppressant for organ recipients. Fungus aside, there are currently well over 120 plant-derived drugs that are enlisted for a whole host of medicinal uses. These include painkillers, laxatives, sedatives, stimulants, expectorants, and muscle relaxants. There are anti-inflammatory, antitumor, anti-cancer, and antimicrobial drugs. These are just a small fraction of the different drug classes that plant-derived pharmaceuticals belong in.

Animals are also highly useful in the medical field. Though some important animal-derived pharmaceuticals are used, they are less numerous than plant-derived ones. Their utility in medicine is mostly serving as experimental animals to test how virulent certain diseases are and to test the effectiveness of drugs. They are also very useful in cooking up antibodies to combat certain diseases. In the past, animals were used to harvest hormones (e.g. insulin) for Type I diabetics, but now with the advent of recombinant DNA technology this is obsolete. We now use bacteria as factories to make human insulin.

I've only scratched the surface of the myriad uses of plants, fungi, and animals in the medical field. But I shouldn't forget to mention some of the medical contributions of two other kingdoms. Bacteria and viruses have been used for centuries to develop vaccines that are effective against many diseases. Even certain kinds of algae have been utilized for their antiviral, antioxidant, and anticancer properties. The list goes on. But someone might say, "Don't we have enough drugs already? Can't we now bypass the drug's original source and synthetically manufacture it if we know the drug's chemical formula?" To some degree, yes, but the medical field will always be searching for new and more effective drugs, particularly ones that have minimal to no side effects. I say let the search continue. But in order to do that we must have all of life's diversity available to explore this living treasury for new discoveries.

DISCUSSION QUESTIONS

1. What should our general attitude be toward food?

2. Besides food, what two substances does the living creation produce that keep us alive and/or healthy?

3. Discuss the restaurant analogy with regard to biodiversity as a global pantry.

9. CREATION: THE GREAT RECYCLER

He loads the thick cloud with moisture;
the clouds scatter his lightning.
They turn around and around by his guidance,
to accomplish all that he commands them
on the face of the habitable world.

ELIHU

JOB 37:11–12

PLANTS AND ANIMALS ARE NOT THE only parts of the creation that God wants us to care for and preserve. Indeed many Christians are woefully un-informed about other important aspects of the creation, particularly what scientists call biogeochemical cycles. I advise that one shouldn't weigh in on some hot environ-mental topic if one doesn't know the first thing about how certain types of matter cycle between the biosphere and atmosphere. If one is ignorant and speaks on these topics, there is a maxim that comes to my mind: "Better to remain silent and be thought a fool, than to speak and remove all doubt." Now, it may seem complicated, but there is a way to know what's going on in broad brush strokes without getting too technical.

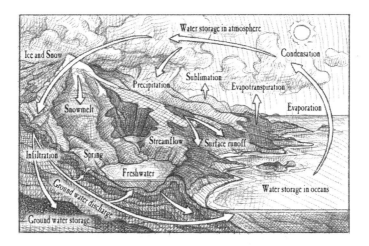

I will briefly summarize three of these biogeochemical cycles: water, carbon, and nitrogen. Let's begin with the water cycle, which you probably already know. Water remains water throughout the cycle but it changes states (solid, liquid, or gas) and geographical location. When liquid water evaporates it becomes water vapor. As it moves up into the atmosphere it cools and condenses into tiny droplets which collectively are called clouds. If the droplets grow big enough, they fall to the earth as rain, snow, hail, etc. This water can run over and through the land and plants and out again. It can run over and through animals and people (and their homes and factories) and out again. Sooner or later it evaporates from some place to start the cycle over again.

Although this is a phenomenon simple enough to learn in grammar school, it's worth pondering as an adult when we consider our divinely-mandated management of it. Fast or slow, water is always on the move. It defies national, state, and private boundaries. Since water inevitably flows from "us" to "them" we must take care that our outgoing water is as good as our incoming water, or at least not harmful for man, animals, and plants by the time it is used. Since we are very accomplished at fouling water in countless ways, it is of paramount importance for us to love our neighbors by taking full responsibility for it being clean before it gets to others. Water is an immense gift from God, but we all share it, use it, and re-use it on a local to global scale. Our dominion responsibilities include water care because *all* life depends on it. The Scriptures say, "And whoever gives one of these little ones even a cup of cold water because he is a disciple, truly, I say to you, he will by no means lose his reward" (Matt. 10:42). Think about it: if by that man's irresponsible actions that cup of water is not fit to drink, I dare say he will lose his reward. I don't think I'm on skinny branches theologically to judge how drinkable these cups of water are, especially at a societal level. God bless wastewater treatment plants that take their job seriously! There are many complex issues surrounding water use that are beyond the scope of this book. However, I hope that I have addressed the basic principles surrounding the issue. Water rights, for instance, can be very difficult and complex to adjudicate, but absolute biblical principles, like property rights and the golden rule, "Love your neighbor as yourself," are essential starting points in solving any water disputes. Without absolute principles the issues get infinitely more complex, and they become hard to resolve by changeable and fallible man-made decrees.

The second important biogeochemical cycle we should be informed about is the carbon cycle. It is much more complex than the water cycle because carbon is an element that is contained in many different kinds of molecules as it continually cycles from the atmosphere to the biosphere and back to the atmosphere. However, you are familiar with part of it already, since most of the carbon in the atmosphere is in the form of carbon dioxide (CO_2), and you probably know that you exhale it. But it's not just a gaseous waste product; it is an essential ingredient for food production. How so? Carbon dioxide plus water is taken into plants and, through the magic of photosynthesis, is made into sugar with the help of sunlight. From the basic sugar molecule (glucose) the plant can then manufacture a variety of biomolecules such as oils, parts of DNA, RNA, proteins, and much more. So, the plants that people and animals eat are either built into their flesh and bone or burned for energy. Even carnivores who don't eat plants have to eat animals that eat plants (or they have to eat animals that eat animals that eat plants). So all food (used either for energy or for constructing and replenishing our bodies) ultimately comes from plants, and most of what plants make their body from is thin air.

Did you know that most of the food you eat doesn't exit your body as solid waste? Rather, it is literally fuel that you burn in all your cells. The waste is released to your bloodstream, carried to your lungs, and exhaled. Yes, our mouths and noses are our exhaust pipes; the same goes for animals. It's a good clean burn, though: you're exhaling CO_2 and water which used to be the bulk of bread, beef, and butter. Let's not forget the solid waste (though we wish we could) which is also part of the carbon cycle. Solid waste is consumed by countless microbes for their growth and energy. They too build their itty-bitty bodies with it, or burn it and release it back into the atmosphere as CO_2 and water. Once there, it can be taken back into plants to start it all over again. As already mentioned, plants release oxygen as a waste product of photosynthesis. Conveniently, this is the very substance we use to burn our food.

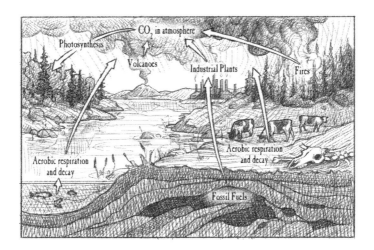

This foundational knowledge is critical to keep in mind when we make carbon-based products. Much of our entrepreneurial spirit is driven by the desire to make useful products and maximize our profit margins. Entrepreneurs rarely if ever have a malicious intent toward the environment, but if they aren't being environmentally circumspect, there can be horrid ecological fallout, from dangerous levels of toxic carbon emissions (like carbon monoxide) to burgeoning plastic wastes that find their way to our oceans. This marine plastic flotsam and jetsam bobbing about in our oceans is more than just unsightly; it has negatively impacted 267 species worldwide through ingestion, starvation, suffocation, infection, drowning, and entanglement.[18] Regardless of whether this has caused a serious decline in any of these species, it is still something we should want to stop. Thankfully efforts are being made to make plastics more biodegradable (more easily consumed by microbes and released back into the atmosphere). Misplaced plastics is not a reason to demonize them. They are very beneficial if used and kept in their proper place. However, once plastics are discarded, it behooves us to make sure they don't find their way to our terrestrial or aquatic ecosystems. Making our plastics biodegradable so that they can be used as food by microbes is a worthy goal. That way plastics are biologically burned and released back into the atmosphere as CO_2. Much work has been done to produce bioplastics. At present the results are a mixed bag (no pun intended), but it seems the pros outweigh the cons.[19] Nevertheless, any cons should spur us on to improve bio-plastics.

Which brings us to another point. Global warming alarmists would have us believe that carbon dioxide is innately bad, and if we put more of it into the atmosphere it will spell global doom. Not so! It's plant food. It will green the planet. I'm all for making our factory and car

18. D.W. Laist, "Impacts of marine debris," in *Marine Debris: Sources, Impacts, and Solutions*, ed. J.M. Coe, and D.B. Rogers, D.B. (New York: Springer-Verlag, 1997), 99–139.

19. Precision Engineered Products Connecticut Plastics, "Biodegradable Plastics," http://www.pepctplastics.com/resources/connecticut-plastics -learning-center/biodegradable-plastics/.

emissions cleaner and plastics biodegradable, but CO_2 is not the problem. It is a net good. The more the better. But more on global warming later in chapter 11.

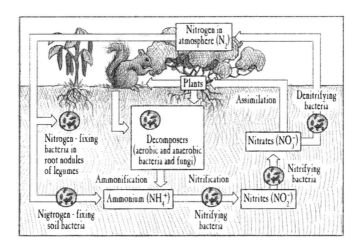

There is one more biogeochemical cycle that is often overlooked by all except farmers and ecologists who study this sort of thing. The nitrogen cycle may seem academic and unnecessary to mention, but it is good for Christians to understand that God created many different microbes, and if they were destroyed, life as we know it would cease. They truly are unsung heroes and it's great to get a general idea of their essential role in sustaining life on earth. To know a little bit about these things may prompt us to be circumspect about how our actions may adversely affect this microbial community, and consequently, the integrity of the nitrogen cycle.

Nitrogen is an element that makes up most of our atmosphere. We don't use it in our respiration, but it is an essential element in the composition of proteins and nucleic acids (DNA & RNA) of all living things, and like water and carbon, it is recycled. Nitrogen gas in the atmosphere is converted into ammonium or ammonia (N_2 → NH_3). This very important conversion, called nitrogen fixation, is accomplished by nitrogen-fixing bacteria in the soil and aquatic ecosystems. Some plants (and certain lichens) fix nitrogen but only because they harbor nitrogen-fixing bacteria within their tissues. Without these bacteria, plants could never get the nitrogen in a form they can use to make proteins and nucleic acids. Plants cannot do anything with N_2. Life would be simply impossible without these bacteria to do this conversion. Without them it would be "nitrogen, nitrogen everywhere and not a drop to drink (for plants)."

Once nitrogen fixation produces ammonia, many plants are still unable to use it. They need other bacteria that convert ammonia into nitrates or nitrites (NO_3 or NO_2). These soil bacteria are called nitrifying bacteria. Nitrate is now in a usable form for plants. Through the plant's biochemical wizardry, the nitrates are converted into a form that can be incorporated into proteins, nucleic acids, and other biomolecules that contain nitrogen (thus becoming part of the plant). When plants are eaten by people and animals, those nitrogen-containing molecules are then incorporated into their flesh, and so on through the food chain. When plants and animals die, decomposers (bacteria and fungi) accomplish another conversion called *ammonification*. This conversion breaks nitrogen-containing organic matter (proteins, nucleic acids, etc.) into ammonia and ammonium where *nitrifying bacteria* can again convert it into nitrates or nitrites (the forms usable by plants). Any excess nitrates or nitrites that aren't absorbed by plants can be converted back into atmospheric nitrogen (N_2) by yet other bacteria called *denitrifying bacteria*. They handily convert nitrates or nitrites into nitrogen gas (N_2). Now we are back to the start.

This is no biology textbook, so why am I bringing all this up? Because mankind was commanded to take dominion, and if we don't know about the organisms that God created to keep our planet alive or functioning properly, then it is easy to inadvertently disturb or destroy ecosystems by just going about our business. As Christians we should want to take dominion responsibly, not ignorantly and recklessly. The more we interact with the natural world, the more informed biologists and non-biologists should be about its interdependency and its life supporting properties.

Wouldn't we think it shameful if the director of a physical plant of some big university knew next to nothing of its computer networks or electrical, mechanical, and heating systems on campus? What if he's a godly Christian? Should we assume all will go well based on that fact? No. God uses means, and a major means He uses is men with knowledge and competence. If a plant director knows next to nothing and manages accordingly, the campus infrastructure will implode. Christians too often just take the natural world for granted as if it were a lovely stage with props and backdrop on which we Christians act out the play of life. We may think the stage crew is responsible to attend to the maintenance of the stage, props, and technical equipment of the environment in which the cast performs the play. Actually, we Christians should be the first to take responsibility for all of this. We can be shamefully apathetic if our activities disturb or destroy an ecosystem, like a rock star who trashes his hotel room knowing full well somebody else will clean it up.

God put Adam in the garden to work it and keep it even before the Fall (Gen. 2:15). Nature is amazingly durable and resilient and though it can sustain itself without our help, God commanded us to tend it and keep it. Christianity should produce leaders in ecology but alas, we have not. Rather than taking the lead, we become reactionary cranks and criticize secular leaders for their wrong-headed worldview and the inane environmental policies that spring from it. Warnings about environmental care, protection of endangered species, etc., can too often be shrugged off by us as nonproblems because nature's most outspoken advocates are often eco-tyrants. I don't defend their ideology, but some of the problems they see are real problems. True, they may wrongly idolize nature and assume that disrupting it is sacrilegious. Just because they are Darwinists or pantheistic idolaters doesn't mean we are incapable of causing serious environmental problems. If we criticize their way of solving these problems yet don't practice a biblical alternative, we are like the woman who was critical of D.L. Moody's evangelistic methods. Once he found out she didn't evangelize, he replied to her, "I like my way of doing it better than your way of not doing it." Secular environmentalists could say the same to us regarding our criticisms of them.

In chapter 12 we will address the major problems (or perceived problems) and consider some possible solutions. We must make distinctions between ill-informed eco-zealots who exaggerate, distort, and sensationalize environmental problems *and* clear-thinking, level-headed ecologists who know how nature works. We need to give serious consideration to the latter and ignore the former. Yes, the eco-zealots too often cry wolf. Sometimes there is no wolf, and sometimes they exaggerate the size of the wolf, but we must keep our eyes peeled for actual wolves. Both of these groups may not admit it, but deep down they assume and behave like humans who know they are responsible to take care of nature for the well-being of both mankind and wildlife. In the same way, a non-Christian contractor may be better at building a house than an incompetent contractor who is a nice, conservative Christian. Many non-Christians can be more competent at gardening, car mechanics, financial planning, engineering, home maintenance, etc. than many Christians. If so, then we should humbly learn from them if they are more gifted at it than we are. However, we need to adopt their know-how without adopting their worldview. We must sort the baby from the bathwater.

DISCUSSION QUESTIONS

1. How can a basic understanding of how nature's biogeochemical cycles enhance how we exercise our dominion responsibilities? (Recall the example of a physical plant director and his knowledge of the university.)

2. What should we learn from secular ecologists and what should we avoid? In other words, what's the baby and what's the bathwater?

10. BIODIVERSITY'S BENEFITS

And God said, "Behold, I have given you every plant yielding
seed that is on the face of all the earth, and every tree with seed
in its fruit. You shall have them for food."

GENESIS 1:29

"Every moving thing that lives shall be food for you. And as I
gave you the green plants, I give you everything."

GENESIS 9:3

IN THIS CHAPTER, I WANT TO WORK
through a few major reasons why I think God created
such enormous variety of life. Knowing my own limitations, I don't dare say this is an exhaustive list, but I
think we will cover most of it. Since this book is about
biblical dominion, you might wonder why I'm focusing

so much on biodiversity conservation. The reason for this is quite simple. The diversity God created is foundational to the integrity of nature as a whole. If a car mechanic wants to exercise proper dominion over a car, it is of utmost importance that he maintain all its parts. He does not throw them away or rearrange them helter-skelter, particularly in the engine. In *A Sand County Almanac*, Aldo Leopold quips, "Who but a fool would discard seemingly useless parts? To keep every cog and wheel is the first precaution of intelligent tinkering."[20] Biodiversity conservation should be our first order of business. I realize that nature is more flexible than car machinery, but even though we can be more creative in arranging the parts, we still need to be well informed while exercising dominion. There are numerous examples of invasive plants and animals that have wrought or are wreaking havoc on natural ecosystems and where we are not able to keep the unwanted guest under control.

I have grouped these benefits in six categories: Resources, Resiliency, Recycling, Recreation, Research, and Restoration.

RESOURCES

I have already addressed this in chapter 8, but in short biodiversity provides for most of our survival needs, like

20. Leopold and Schwartz, 190.

food and oxygen and much of our needs like clothing, shelter, and pharmaceuticals.

RESILIENCY

A number of studies in a variety of different ecosystems have shown that higher biodiversity makes the ecosystem more resilient. In other words, ecosystems that are species rich tend to bounce back after being perturbed or damaged by say a hurricane, wildfire, clear-cut, etc. It makes sense. The greater the number of species inhabiting an area, the greater the likelihood that each species will be more successful at leaving a remnant that survives perturbation, whether it's seeds, root systems, or animals that may have fled from the catastrophe but migrated back once it was over. If the ecosystem has fewer species, there is less of a chance of having a remnant of each species to reestablish the community. Also, more species usually means more mutualistic relationships, where two species are in a mutually beneficial partnership. That means areas of high biodiversity have more relationships where the species involved help each other get re-established after a disaster.

Here's an analogy that might clarify. Suppose there is a healthy community with many family ties and strong friendships. Another community is just a big as the first but has few family ties and few strong friendships. If both communities are hit by tornadoes and each had the same number of fatalities and property damage, which will bounce back more quickly?

RECYCLING (THE KIND NATURE DOES)

I don't need to reiterate this idea here since I covered it in chapter 9. However, I will underscore the importance of many seemingly unimportant animals, plants, fungi, bacteria, and other microbes. Many are involved in the aforementioned and essential biogeochemical cycles and keep life alive at a global scale. I only discussed three cycles earlier, but there are others that are just as important. To eliminate certain species, whether inadvertently or on purpose, before we actually know what they do, is folly, pure and simple. I don't know much about my car engine, but I certainly don't yank out random car parts to lighten my car or because I don't like their looks. You'd think I was crazy to assume that if I don't know what it does, it probably does nothing. There are car parts that aren't essential (if you remove the seat cushions it will still run), but the manufacturer still put them there for good reason. We must have a similar mentality when it comes to biodiversity. God gave us the luxury edition of global diversity. Some animals and plants may not be essential, but they are simply wonderful. Bamboo forests in China can survive without pandas, but why not have both? God's command is to rule over them. That means study, beautify, utilize, manage, and enjoy them. This is all part of good dominion, but removing them is not. Extirpation and/or extinction is just bad dominion.

We don't need to be experts in all of this stuff, but if we are ignorant, we should at least be good listeners to those experts who do know a good deal more than we do about biodiversity and the myriad roles of living organisms. Experts or not, it is very prudent to be circumspect about how our activities may impact the environment and the many life forms that exists therein. Let's keep this thing intact.

RECREATION

Taking wise dominion over nature isn't just about keeping the ship afloat; it is also about enjoying the cruise. Apart from the many utilitarian reasons for maintaining the created diversity through godly dominion, there is still ample reason to maintain it simply because it is delightful, interesting, beautiful, and spectacular. There are countless recreational activities that require the healthy existence of many species. Think of all the delights people have experienced throughout world history with pets. God didn't make one kind of animal for our general pet needs. In talking about taming the tongue, James 3:7–8 says, "For every kind of beast and bird, of reptile and sea creature, can be tamed and has been tamed by mankind, but no human being can tame the tongue." God didn't give us restrictions on taming animals. There are typical conventional pets (cats and dogs), but there are also countless creatures of manageable size that people have figured out how to keep healthy in captivity if they have the space, time, and money. Zoos were created for the public to enjoy those animals that are beyond the resources of individual pet owners.

How about boating? Would you like to boat around a lake whose shores and water had no life? Probably not. Would you like to go on a Caribbean cruise where there were no coral reefs or reef fish? Or an Alaskan cruise with no whales or seals? Would you like to hike where there were no trees, wildflowers, or wildlife? Would you like to fish or pretend to fish? Would you like to hunt or pretend to hunt? Would you rather go to the zoo or thumb through a book on extinct animals? We often take many of these pleasures for granted until some sudden or gradual environmental crisis ends or diminishes them. And don't assume that domesticated animals and plants that are directly under our protection are immune to environmental crises. Droughts, pandemics, infestations, and pollution affect more than wildlife. Maybe the western North American bark beetle infestation doesn't directly affect the welfare of your Pekingese, but indirect effects can always happen if the crisis is big enough. What is keeping everything propped up on a larger scale? God, of course. But God uses *means,* and, regarding the existence of life, that means is man's wise and obedient dominion over it. That is what enables all of us to keep enjoying these things.

RESEARCH

Besides resiliency, recycling, and recreation, the manifold blessings of life's variety have been a great boon to research. The extreme diversity stimulates our curiosity in a variety of ways. God made people with an enormous array of interests. This is particularly true for biologists, who are a motley crew and whose research interests and curiosities are many and diverse. They may span different levels of biological organization from the molecular to the ecosystem level. For example, ecologists like studying natural interactions between organisms and the environment, whereas molecular biologists like studying the interactions between molecules in a cell. Other biologists are not as interested in the particular level as in a particular group. Botanists like plants, ornithologists like birds, herpetologists like amphibians and reptiles, bacteriologists like bacteria, and so on. God's creation is diverse enough to cover the field of all possible biological research interests. A sparse creation limited to a handful of necessary kinds would not have piqued the curiosity and hooked most of those people who are currently biologists. Biodiversity is like a smorgasbord for would-be biologists. There is something for every inclination. That doesn't mean they all have their dream job, but nevertheless the copious variety has led to much more fruitful research than if life's diversity was minimal. Let's consider a few.

The great pioneers in microbiology, Louis Pasteur and Robert Koch, gave us the germ theory of disease and other advances in vaccinations and immunology. There are now thousands of microbiologists making great discoveries in medicine, genetics, ecology, and a host of other subdisciplines in microbiology. Marine biologists studying the huge variety of sea creatures—ranging from sponges, jellyfish, sea stars, fish, and whales—have added much to our understanding of physiology, embryological development, biochemistry, ecology, and genetics. Mammalogists studying bats and whales have unveiled the phenomenal physiology of echolocation along with its practical applications in sonar. Biomedical science, driven by the humanitarian desire to help the sick and infirm, has led to countless discoveries that have increased human health, quality of life, and longevity. Ornithologists have recently made great strides in understanding the magnetic compass in migratory birds. Ornithologists also researching the extraordinary hearing in certain birds have opened doors to new solutions for hearing loss. Research on the vision of raptors has also provided new insights in optical design. Even outside of the obviously practical fields of agricultural and biomedical science, many discoveries have created a booming field called biomimetics. Life's incredible diversity holds an almost inexhaustible supply of ingeniously designed biological gadgetry. Clever scientists interested in this field are throwing a lot of brain power at imitating and incorporating divine designs to create new or improve existing products. In keeping with His generosity, God didn't patent it; it's free for the taking. Without this overwhelming diversity, much of what we currently know would still be shrouded in mystery simply because a limited array of utilitarian species like corn, cattle, and cane wouldn't have ginned up the same kind of curiosity or possibilities that God's lavish creation has.

RESTORATION

Habitat restoration isn't exactly a benefit, but it's appropriate to address here because it seeks to regain the loss of biodiversity benefits due to habitat destruction. We have done a lot of damage in the last few centuries to the environment, most of it after the industrial revolution. Some well-known examples of animals we've stupidly thrown under the bus are the dodo bird of Mauritius Island in the Indian Ocean, the Tasmanian wolf, the moa on New Zealand, the passenger pigeon in North America, the Carolina parakeet in the southeast U.S., and many more. We've gone a long ways toward rubbing others out, but surprisingly they have survived our reckless ravages so far. Nevertheless, many are currently on the brink of extinction, and many committed conservation biologists (usually secular folks with a naturalistic worldview) are working tirelessly to maintain their rightful place on earth.[21] This reminds me of Romans 2:14-15: "For when Gentiles, who do not have the law, by nature do what the law requires, they are a law to themselves, even though they do not have the law. They show that the work of the law is written on their hearts, while their conscience also bears witness, and their conflicting thoughts accuse or even excuse them." Thankfully many countries are learning from their mistakes, both minor and major. Our government has adopted legislation that is cleaning up our water and air (the Clean Water Act and the Clean Air Act). We are trying to protect endangered species (Endangered Species Act). Our government is charged to make industries comply with environmental regulations regarding pollution and hazardous waste, and is making developers jump through hoops by requiring them to write up environmental impact statements (EIS) or environmental assessments (EA). These are efforts to make a developer look hard at the consequences and costs of their construction. These environmental policies have been at best a mixed bag, but I don't want to itemize and niggle about their problems. Their goals were and are, in the main, good. However, trying to impose environmental regulations on a chafing public, no matter how good and well-intentioned they are, is dealing with the symptoms, not getting at the cause. Even

21. Jane Goodall et al., *Hope for Animals and Their World: How Endangered Species Are Being Rescued from the Brink* (New York: Grand Central Pub, 2011).

assuming good policies, top-down command and control tactics are generally ineffective if the public at large doesn't give a rip about this or that endangered species, or could care less about the pollution they generate or about the health of this or that habitat. The best strategy is to first reconcile people to God by means of preaching the Gospel. This at first blush doesn't seem to be addressing any particular environmental problem, but it actually is. Most problems, environmental or not, can be traced back to some kind of sin. Repentance and forgiveness by God deal with sin, digging it up by the root. Many sins have either direct or indirect connections to environmental problems, and so reconciling people to the Creator will in time reconcile people to the creation. As Francis Schaeffer cogently pointed out in his book *Pollution and the Death of Man,*

> If things are treated only as autonomous machines, in a decreated world, they are finally meaningless . . . But if individually and in the Christian community I treat with integrity the things which God has made, and treat them this way lovingly, because they are His, things *change*. If I love the Lover, I love what the Lover has made.[22]

My desire is to instill in all my Christian brothers and sisters a love for the Creator. This is impossible unless

22. Page 93.

they are first reconciled to Him, and reconciliation with God is only accomplished through the Gospel. Not necessarily overnight, but in time as we come to a deeper knowledge and love of God, our knowledge and desire to care for the creation will grow. Once love for God is in our bones, effective methodologies of wise dominion will emerge sooner rather than later.

So how do we go about reclaiming a destroyed habitat, or how do we save animals from the brink of extinction? First, this is not a how-to book. There are many resources out there that provide detailed methodologies about fixing environments we've broken or saving endangered species. My goal here is to lay out biblical principles to help shape how we view God's glorious creation. This, in turn, should affect decisions about how we treat it. Methodologies are needed if our decision requires some action. To solve environmental problems, one needs to get really educated on the particulars.

So, say you decide to restore a degraded ecosystem. Such a task can be compared to first aid on a badly skinned knee. You remove any bad stuff such as gravel or dirt, soothe and disinfect it by adding ointments or antibiotics, and cover it up with a bandage so it is protected from further insults. It will heal itself. Too much intervention isn't necessarily a good thing. It is the same with the environment: our well-meaning efforts to clean up the Exxon Valdez oil spill may have done more harm than good.[23] Some medical procedures like neurosurgery require many years of advanced education and training. Most habitat restoration is more like first aid. In the same way, we first figure out what shouldn't be there and what should be there. The latter include native plants and animals that need to be repatriated. We remove, if possible, the unwanted non-native species (i.e. the invasive and weedy ones). If they aren't particularly a problem and can coexist with the native flora and fauna, there is no need to spend an inordinate amount of effort and money trying to remove them. We then reintroduce the correct species in the right quantities and then, apart from monitoring the reintroduction progress, leave it alone. Habitats, if given the right mix of native species and some outside help, will more or less heal themselves.

All this may not require a Ph.D., but it does require a lot of homework, commitment, and fieldwork. If we are trying to save a species from extinction we need to do a lot of research. We need to find out the animal's ecological niche (lifestyle or profession). This includes what specific habitat is required, what it feeds on, what its movement patterns and nesting requirements are, etc. Homework, homework, homework. To save a species may also require a lot of money and/or time in order to first reclaim the habitat it needs. Captive breeding

23. Bryan Walsh, "Should the Oil Spill Be Left to Spill," *Time*, June 29, 2010, http://science.time.com/2010/06/29/should-the-oil-spill-be-left-to-spill/.

efforts are usually needed to build up a decent number of animals that could be effectively released. Natural reproduction in the wild may not be feasible due to poor animal density and poor habitat quality; you shouldn't just release too few animals into an unsuitable habitat.

Again, the above overview isn't meant to be a how-to guide, but is meant to give you a notion that restoration can require a lot of research, work, time, and money. It is generally not a project for a single property owner, unless it is reclaiming a backyard pond. This is almost always a group effort.

To get an idea of what's involved in rescuing animals on the brink of extinction, read *Hope for Animals and Their World* by Jane Goodall. In referring to secular works, I want to be clear that I don't advocate the worldviews contained therein. It is often clear that the value of endangered species is idolized, and made equal to or exalted above human value. That's the bathwater to be tossed. However, insofar as they are trying to save a good thing, we frankly applaud the effort and can learn a lot about how they do it; that's the baby to keep.

DISCUSSION QUESTIONS

1. What are the first five main benefits to biodiversity? Briefly explain each.

2. What are the three basic steps in habitat restoration?

PART 3: PROBLEMS AND SOLUTIONS

11. CHRISTIANITY IS THE SOLUTION, NOT THE PROBLEM

The Christian is a man who has a reason for dealing with

each created thing with a high level of respect.

FRANCIS A. SCHAEFFER[24]

IN *POLLUTION AND THE DEATH OF MAN*, Francis Schaeffer includes a couple essays in his appendix to show what we are up against. One by Lynn White Jr. called "The Historical Roots of Our Ecologic Crisis" gives a brief survey of how religion and philosophy shape our relationship to nature. He eventually lays most of the blame for our current ecological problems at the feet of Christianity. In describing man's relationship to creation, White says, "God planned all of this explicitly for

24. *Pollution and the Death of Man*, 55.

man's benefit and rule: no item in the physical creation had any purpose save to serve man's purposes. And, although man's body is made of clay, he is not simply part of nature: he is made in the image of God."[25] White also explains that the pagan notion of animism meant that if superstitious man modified or partook of nature, i.e. logging, mining, damming a stream, he truly felt that he violated the gods of the trees, earth, and rivers. They therefore needed to be pacified through some kind of oblation. With the spread of the Gospel, there was a shift from an animistic worldview to a Christian worldview; therefore it wasn't necessary to appease any offended deities. Nature was considered only physical, not spiritual.

White goes on to say, "By destroying animism, Christianity made it possible to exploit nature in a mood of indifference to the feelings of natural objects."[26] According to White, the dominion mandate can be viewed as a license to exploit the world's resources without restraint. Without an animistic view of nature, we never have to worry about stepping on the toes of any god: *God put us in charge. Nature's bounty is free for the taking. God told us to fill and subdue the earth so let's get on with it. Let's maximize our profits!* So, is White correct in blaming Christianity?

25. White, "The Historical Roots of Our Ecologic Crisis," *Science*, New Series, 155, no. 3767 (1967): 1205.
26. Ibid.

I freely admit that Christians are sinners and have participated in pillaging the environment along with much of Western culture, but Christianity is not the problem, because greed is not Christian. White argues that ecological crises were largely due to a Christian view of dominion and a nexus between science and technology, both of which rose from a Christian view of nature. It is true that science and technology arose from Christianity. Nancy Pearcey clearly documents that the Christian worldview was indeed the rich soil from which Western science and technology grew.[27] This claim is not tenuous. Even White acknowledges the fact. He writes, "Our science and technology have grown out of Christian attitudes toward man's relation to nature which are almost universally held not only by Christians and neo-Christians but also by those who fondly regard themselves as post-Christians."[28] Unfortunately, he commits the guilt by association fallacy. Let's put it in a syllogism.

1. The Christian worldview produced science and technology.

2. Science and technology produced tools that can cause great ecological damage.

27. N. R. Pearcey, *The Soul of Science: Christian Faith and Natural Philosophy* (Wheaton, IL: Crossway Books, 1994).
28. White, 1206.

3. Therefore, the Christian worldview is to be blamed for man-made ecological crises.

Science and technology are great blessings, but there are countless ways to unlawfully use them. Give a man a gun, and if lawfully used, it can be a blessing to him and others (he can fill his freezer with venison and share it with others). But if he hates his neighbor, he can use his gun to murder him. Murder is not in the heart of a gun; it's in the heart of man. This distinction is very important because it is true with every tool. We can use the internet for great good or for great evil. Conversely, we can use a walkie-talkie for little good or little evil. We can use a bulldozer for great good or great evil, and a stone hoe for little good or little evil. It all boils down to whether we love God or not. Science and technology are powerful tools that grew from a Christian soil. Science and technology can help multiply and magnify evil, but the Christian worldview wasn't the cause of the evil. Put into the hands of sinful, greedy, covetous, and idolatrous men, the fruits of science and technology can be turned to wicked uses.

Matthew 12:35: "The good person out of his good treasure brings forth good, and the evil person out of his evil treasure brings forth evil." Greed and covetousness plus Stone Age animistic culture can result in headhunting or cannibalistic feuds. Greed and covetousness plus the fruits of science and technology can result in genocides, over 1.5 billion abortions worldwide since 1980, unrestrained habitat destruction, air that is not fit to breathe, polluted rivers and lakes, and extinction of God's creatures. Although Lynn White is not suggesting we ditch modern science, he wrongly assumes that the dominion mandate is inherently destructive to the environment. The only teachings in the Christian tradition that Lynn White seemed to appreciate was Saint Francis of Assisi's.[29] But since Saint Francis's teachings didn't prevail in mainstream Christianity, White suggests that we should pursue a post-Christian view of nature. Unfortunately, in his essay he fails to see the fundamental problem, which is wickedness in the heart of man, not the dominion mandate or the tools man uses to magnify his wickedness.

CHRISTIANITY IS THE ANSWER

"Like a sparrow in its flitting, like a swallow in its flying, a curse that is causeless does not alight" (Prov. 26:2).

As I explained above, Christians can act wrongly toward the environment. But the actual teachings of the Christian faith cannot be charged with the current environmental problems. Yes, Christians can be a problem, but not if they understand and practice dominion in a thoroughly Christian way. But I'm not satisfied with

29. White, 1206.

just refuting White's claim that Christianity is guilty; I want to turn the tables. Disobedient Christians may be culpable for their participation in environmental exploitation, but truly biblical dominion rightly practiced cannot be blamed for damage done to the environment. In fact, biblical dominion is the only coherent long-term solution to these problems. No other world religion or philosophy has an absolute moral standard to even address the problems. In order for a religion or philosophy to have any traction or foothold to address any environmental problem, it must have some kind of fixed standard of right or wrong, goodness or badness.

Darwinism is the easiest philosophy to demonstrate how bankrupt it is with regard to environmental ethics, or any other ethics for that matter. Let's put the argument in uncomplicated prose. If naturalism is true, then there is no supreme, transcendent Being; there is only matter, energy, time, and chance. Therefore, the universe and all that's in it is the result of mindless matter being shaped by purposeless forces over eons of time. If that is true, there is no absolute basis for right or wrong, good or bad, beauty or ugliness, since mindless matter cannot generate any kind of absolute standard—moral, aesthetic, or otherwise. If nature is all there is, then whatever happens happens. There are no "rules of the game." There are no "fouls." There are no "penalties." There is no "out of bounds." Why? There is no Cosmic Referee.

If no one designed the game, there can be no statement like, "It ought to happen this way," or "It should happen that way." Instead, nature is aimless, meaningless, and valueless. A mushroom has no more or less meaning than a man.

If a naturalist claims to have a standard, it is (like everything else under the umbrella of naturalistic evolution) completely subject to change (and that's not really a standard) due to the ebb and flow of humanity's collective whim. That's why I think it's so hilarious when thoroughgoing naturalists get so angry about the possible extinction of some amazing animal or plant. They have much zeal, commitment, and purpose to save some species they value, but their worldview provides them with no basis for any of it. Why do they bustle about in righteous indignation at the possible loss of a species? They may love the animal or plant but others (likely the majority) may love money more. What if the majority doesn't really care about some species going extinct? How do we judge which love is the right love? Democracy? How do we know democracy is right? By vote? But voting presupposes the rightness of democracy. Hmmm. When a Darwinist sees that something has gone wrong, he must adopt a soap box to launch a conservation crusade from another worldview (one that actually has absolutes) simply because consistent Darwinism doesn't and can't have absolutes. Darwinism, which is naturalistic in its assumptions, has no answers for anything. Darwinism can't teach "This ought to be"; it can only teach "This is." If Darwinism is true, all cognitive thought, opinions, and emotions (including logic, justice, wisdom, love, compassion, mercy, and even the concept of truth) are reduced to various neurochemical reactions in the brain. By the way, how do we judge which set of neurochemical reactions are the best or the fittest? In a Darwinian world, judgment itself is just another set of neurochemical reactions. So, you have to use one set of neurochemical reactions to assess the legitimacy of other neurochemical reactions. There has to be a standard outside of this huge array of neurochemical reactions to make any true judgment.

Despite a worldview with no absolutes, many Darwinists are still very opinionated. Darwinists can be some of the most opinionated, indignant, dogmatic people I've ever seen. This is because they deeply hold views that appear, well, absolute. If they were consistent with their naturalistic premise (which is itself yet another neurochemical reaction in a Darwinian world), they would see their mental (neurochemical) state as having no more biological significance than a stomachache. They would see that their vehement thoughts against extinction are simply an agitated set of neurochemical reactions which occur under these ecological circumstances. If naturalism is true, their opinions are completely based on a set of neurochemical reactions ultimately determined by their genetics, upbringing, diet, climate, etc. and should be held accordingly, that is, with a grain of salt. Their opinions have no more weight or value than anybody else's opinion who may have completely different genetics, upbringing, diet, climate, etc.

Pantheism (including all its ancient and current manifestations) does not believe in a god that is transcendent or distinct from the creation. Their god is indistinguishable from the universe. Therefore we, along with everything else, are part of god. The following are various religions and philosophies that are either clearly pantheistic or are a mixture of it and other doctrines: African tribal religions, North American tribal religions, Sikhism, Taoism, Confucianism, and Hinduism. This chapter is not a comparative religions summary, so I will not look at their distinctives to contrast or compare them. Pantheism's perennial problem has been solving the problem of evil. If everything can be conflated with god and god can be conflated with everything, then bad things like cancer, tsunamis, human cruelty, pollution, extinction, you name it, are all manifestations of god. Is god good or bad or both? If both, then technically speaking the problem of evil is a problem with god. If you fight evil, then you are fighting against god or at least a part of god, i.e. nature, the universe. So how does a pantheist tease out the good bits and make them distinct from the bad bits? They really can't and be a consistent pantheist. In *Star Wars*, "The Force" is Hollywood's attempt at a pantheistic god. But in order to have good guys be really good and bad guys be really bad, the creators had to make the Light Side of the Force distinct from the Dark Side. If they hadn't, the movie probably would have failed. When I had my elderly mom watch *Star Wars*, I had to explain that the stormtroopers were bad guys even though their armor was white. In the same way, in consistent pantheism you really can't separate good and evil. It's all mixed up as exemplified in Yin and Yang. Opposite, antagonistic forces are inseparable, interconnected, and interdependent. This is in stark contrast with Christianity. In Deuteronomy 32:4 speaking of God, Moses writes,

> The Rock, his work is perfect,
>> for all his ways are justice.
> A God of faithfulness and without iniquity,
>> just and upright is he.

Similarly, James 1:17 says, "Every good gift and every perfect gift is from above, coming down from the Father of lights, with whom there is no variation or shadow due to change."

Similarly, we know that evil comes from below, coming up from the father of darkness. The Christian God is not Yin and Yang.

This and many other passages make it very clear that the transcendent God of the Bible, the Creator of all, is untainted by sin. He is holy, righteous, and perfect in all His attributes. Only created man and other creatures are twisted, bent, and ruined by sin.

Let's look at Buddhism, even though it's a type of pantheism, because it's a major world religion. Most of us know that Buddhism "in principle" is friendly to the environment, but does it provide any foundation for an environmental ethic? I use the principle loosely here since Buddhism is very nebulous. Buddhism follows the teachings of Buddha since it is presumed that he was a very enlightened person. However, it does not acknowledge a supreme Creator of any sort, and therefore there aren't any binding commandments given to mankind from divine authority. It assumes that when one is enlightened, he or she will just know the good and do it. Killing of anything—man, animal, or plant—is frowned upon, just because killing is not very nice. This Disneyesque ethic of Buddhism is therefore considered green. This is a pretty naive position to maintain. In a fallen world, even in beautiful, balanced, and unpolluted ecosystems, killing of countless creatures occurs (whether we or natural predators do the job). In fact, for our fallen world to remain beautiful and balanced, it must occur. Wildlife management methods often do involve culling herds, which involves killing invasive species or other animals whose populations have gotten out of hand, especially when there aren't natural predators to do the job.[30] Why is it wrong for people to do the killing but not other animals?

In short, Buddhism does not provide any absolute foundation to their moral system since there are no commandments given to mankind from any divine being. The best they can do is say killing is frowned upon. But who is doing the frowning? What kind of authority does the frowner have? Why is it frowned upon? Should I feel guilty if I'm frowned at? Do non-human predators get frowned at? If they don't, why the double standard? How come man can't be a predator or omnivore? Does getting frowned at by other Buddhists generate legitimate guilt, or is it just negative peer pressure? Even if they provide answers to these questions, it is clear that their environmental ethic is not binding.

Although there are other religions or philosophies and many distinctions between them, the ones that follow are the only ones that hold to a transcendent Creator. Some are old and some are young. Judaism is the root of the Christian faith and so predates it. But because it rejects Jesus Christ, the fulfillment of the Old Testament, it is a heresy. However, because it

30. National Park Service, "Park Deer Management Program Will Run October '18 through March '19," August 27, 2018, https://www.nps.gov/gett/learn/news/18-19-deer-management.htm.

is founded on the Old Testament it can embrace the same commands to exercise dominion over the earth. Islam is a much later (seventh century) spin-off from Christianity, founded by Muhammad. Muslims believe in portions of the Old Testament, although they think that the documents we hold to are corrupted. They accept the Torah (first 5 books), the Psalms, and some of the New Testament (the Gospels). These portions of the Bible plus the Quran are what Muslims consider to be the scriptures. However, because they believe in a transcendent Creator of all things, Allah, and believes the parts of the Old Testament that include the dominion mandate, they have an absolute basis for an environmental ethic. There are also a number of verses in the Quran that speak to man's responsibility to the environment. They are similar to the Bible's teaching. Here are a couple:

1. "But seek, through that which Allah has given you, the home of the Hereafter; and [yet], do not forget your share of the world. And do good as Allah has done good to you. And desire not corruption in the land. Indeed, Allah does not like corrupters." (Sahih International, Quran 28:77)

2. "And it is He who has made you successors upon the earth and has raised some of you above others in degrees [of rank] that He may try you through

what He has given you. Indeed, your Lord is swift in penalty; but indeed, He is Forgiving and Merciful." (Sahih International, Quran 6:165).

There are other verses as well. Whether or not Islam exercises dominion well, it does have a foundation for environmental ethics. Similar to the biblical teaching, Allah is believed to charge humankind to be stewards of the creation he has made. A number of Muslim biologists and ecologists have highlighted Quranic verses to foster an environmental and conservation ethic among their fellow Muslims. In all fairness, belief in a divine Creator is the only way one can have any absolutes about anything, so even if we think most Muslims are not very green, we can't therefore claim that the Quran is fundamentally anti-green. We don't want non-Christians to assume the true God of the Bible does not care about His creation by looking at the behavior of many Christians. In the same way, we don't want to speak inaccurately about the teaching of Islam regarding the creation by committing a straw man fallacy. We can honestly say it is a false religion with a false god. My goal here is not to derive an environmental ethic from the Quran; I will defer to a devout Muslim ecologist to do that. My only point here is that it can be done despite the behavior of many Muslims. All Christian cults and heresies (Mormonism, Jehovah's Witness, etc.) are in a similar position regarding the environment. If you believe in a transcendent Creator and also believe the dominion mandate (Gen. 1:28) hasn't been revoked, then you have an absolute doctrinal foundation from which you can derive and practice an environmental ethic.

DISCUSSION QUESTIONS

1. Briefly explain why Darwinism and pantheism cannot provide an absolute ethical standard to solve environmental problems.

2. Why is a personal, infinite, transcendent Creator necessary for the existence of an absolute ethical standard?

12. ENVIRONMENTAL ISSUES AND THE CHRISTIAN

Conservation is a state of harmony between men and land.
By land is meant all of the things on, over, or in the earth.
Harmony with the land is like harmony with a friend; you
cannot cherish his right hand and chop off his left.

ALDO LEOPOLD[31]

IF CHRISTIANITY IS THE ONLY LEGITI-mate foundation for solving environmental problems, why is it that groups with the wrong religion or philosophy are trying much harder to solve them? The short answer is that most people are motivated by their gut, not their brains.

31. A *Sand County Almanac*, 189.

Even though Christianity or Christian heresies are the only religions providing an *absolute* moral foundation for environmental ethics, it is also true that the most active and zealous environmentalists are either thoroughgoing naturalists (Darwinists) or pantheists of some nebulous stripe. What are we to make of it? We have a proper philosophical foundation; they don't, yet people's gut reactions to problems and their passion to do something about it is rarely consistent with their belief system in the abstract. Many people don't even know what they believe, let alone consistently follow the practical outworkings of their belief system. What they do know is that they *love* nature, and if they can get themselves and others whipped up about some perceived or real environmental problem, they can get a movement going. If their crusade gets the government, NGOs, and the scientific establishment behind it, then few people bother questioning the legitimacy of its philosophical underpinnings. It's like trying to stop a tank division at full speed and ask, "What are you doing? Are your papers in order?" The academic community are opportunists. They know when a big culture-wide bandwagon is on the roll. They also know that if they jump on, they are clever and credentialed enough to get in the driver's seat. In other words, they are able to maneuver themselves into a position of power and influence. These movements, in one sense, have the mentality and inertia of the mob. With the scientific community and educated like-minded organizations at the helm, the movement is given a sense of legitimacy. It isn't worth trying to stop them by trying to talk sense or grabbing the helm from them through political muscle power. Apart from the heart-changing power of the Gospel through the conversion of people one by one, it is futile to make desired changes through argumentation, lobbying, and other sorts of political power grabs. I am much more interested in ushering in biblical dominion and biodiversity conservation through the transformation of culture by the Gospel. It will happen like yeast in the loaf. A real grassroots change can happen due to the transforming power of the Gospel. It is described by Francis Schaeffer this way regarding our dislocation with God, fellow men, and nature: "But Christians who believe the Bible are not simply called to say that 'one day' there will be healing, but that by God's grace, upon the basis of the work of Christ, substantial healing can be a reality here and now."[32]

There are many environmental issues today, most of which are paraded by the secular media as reaching crisis levels, i.e. pollution, habitat destruction, extinction of plants and animals, overpopulation, climate change, etc. How can you get people's attention and raise awareness? Cry "Wolf!" of course.

32. Schaeffer and Middlemann, 66.

There are three main steps to doing this effectively. First, identify the environmental problem (real or imagined). Second, whip up a lot of public concern by highlighting the problem through incessant propaganda using every kind of media. The problem is often magnified to enormous proportions to make it appear that our planet hangs in the balance. When people question whether or not the problem is really that big, the experts say this huge problem is subtle and complicated. Only good scientists[33] can detect it and figure out a solution (bad scientists[34] are not clever enough to see the problem, enormous though it is). Third, convince the public that only the State can save us from certain doom. The State is our only savior. You should vote for candidates and legislation that prioritize the problem so we can get to work saving the planet from certain doom. If you vote for the conservative candidate, you are an enemy of the planet and the future happiness of all life on earth.

In all fairness, there are many problems that need our attention, some more than others. Some problems (considered to be global crises) are at most minor problems. In this chapter I want to lay out biblical principles so we

33. Scientists that agree with the State on the existence and magnitude of the problem. They analyze cherry-picked data that accentuates the problem and agree with State-mandated solutions to the problem.

34. Scientists that don't agree with the State on the existence and magnitude of the problem because they analyzed the data objectively and drew conclusions quite different from the "good scientists."

can navigate these troubled waters without being caught up in the hype. My goal is not to quantify the problems using graphs and pie charts, or prioritize problems, or lay out environmental laws that we are violating and admonish us to obey them. That has been done by others who know the facts better than I do. My goal is to pull back the curtain on the secularist agenda so that you will be much more dubious about the veracity of their claims. In some cases they have rightly identified a real problem (though often exaggerated), but their solutions are far from biblical. In some cases they identify something as a huge problem that's actually no problem at all. And of course a solution to a nonproblem can produce other problems. But I don't just want Christians to be deaf to the eco-alarmist rants and go on their merry way. I want Christians to become leaders in how they care for the creation, in how they approach and solve environmental problems, and in how they educate their children about our huge responsibility of taking dominion. We too often react to their unwarranted alarmism by rolling our eyes at them and then doing nothing.

PROBLEM 1: POLLUTION
(OR ANY YUCKY THINGS WE PRODUCE)

Every sane person if given a choice would rather drink clean water and breathe clean air over fouled water and air. So, the dispute is not usually about whether polluted water and air is good, but about the extent of the pollution and how much the industry needs to shell out in mitigating the problem. This book is written to teachable Christians who want to understand their dominion responsibilities better. I doubt I will change the minds of millionaire industrial magnates so that they will repent of their greedy ways and stop damaging the environment. In order to survive, companies must make a profit. Eliminating or reducing the pollution to acceptable levels can be extremely expensive and consequently conflict arises on several fronts: 1) What is an acceptable level? 2) Who decides the acceptable level? 3) How much should I have to pay in compliance costs in order to reduce pollution to those levels? These are big questions, and responsible people who make undesirable waste products while making their desired products should seek to answer them. The easy part is actually quantifying the pollution. The difficult part is how to assess how bad it is and how to deal with it once we've found out.

The biblical principle here is simple. Love your neighbor as yourself. Say you own a big chemical company that produces a number of nasty chemical wastes. As a Christian you should not have the mentality of "What can I legally get away with when dumping it into the air or water?" Rather your first question should be, "How can I love my neighbor with my company, not just my clients by giving them a good product at a good price? How can I work toward redeeming the creation in my business?" Unfortunately, many secular companies are being more ecologically circumspect than Christians are. They may be doing it for PR reasons (they might not particularly care for the environment, but they've figured out that being green attracts more business), but we should still be asking how we can benefit our neighbor in every aspect of our business, not just how we can make a good product. Is your facility an eyesore? If it is, work to make it look aesthetically pleasing as far as you are able. Are you fouling the air and water at legal levels? If you are, work toward not fouling it at all. "Leave it better than you found it" is a good rule of thumb for a Christian whether you're borrowing a lawn mower, camping in the woods, or running a huge factory by the river.

Besides abiding by current environmental regulations like the Clean Water Act, the Clean Air Act, or the Endangered Species Act, consult a level-headed ecologist to see if your company is really good for the health of the region's air and watershed. You may already comply with all environmental legislation, but your mentality should not be just compliance to the letter of the law, but rather loving your neighbor. It may mean more than what the regulations require. This is hard to do especially if you've already complied with it all. Many companies would rather pay the fines because it's less than compliance costs. In business, too often it's about avoiding fines or extra costs, and not about loving your neighbor. "But, alas, my profits will keep dwindling," you say. Ah, but God blesses obedience. Consider Deuteronomy 28:12-14:

> The LORD will open the heavens, the storehouse of his bounty, to send rain on your land in season and to bless all the work of your hands. You will lend to many nations but will borrow from none. The LORD will make you the head, not the tail. If you pay attention to the commands of the LORD your God that I give you this day and carefully follow them, you will always be at the top, never at the bottom. Do not turn aside from any of the commands I give you today, to the right or to the left, following other gods and serving them. (NIV)

Some theological camps claim that these promises are only to the children of Israel in that stage in redemptive history. Even if you don't think these promises are still in effect under the new covenant, we all agree that we are to love our neighbor as ourself. When we fail to love our neighbor as we should and we confess it as sin, Christ's blood cleanses us from it. His grace also enables us to love our neighbor in these very tangible ways. God blesses obedience if it's done in faith. So, promises of physical blessings or not, we are still to love our neighbor.

> For by grace you have been saved through faith. And this is not your own doing; it is the gift of God, not a

result of works, so that no one may boast. For we are his workmanship, created in Christ Jesus for good works, which God prepared beforehand, that we should walk in them. (Eph. 2:8–10)

We often look to the world to show us how to bless ourselves (with more money) rather than how to serve God, care for the creation, and bless our neighbor in tangible and intangible ways. Businessmen often think that they can make more money if they are open seven days a week. We think that if we're open on Sunday we'll get ahead or at least stay in the running. Whether or not we do make more money is not the question that should concern us. We think we shouldn't give our farmland a Sabbath rest. Why forgo a year's worth of produce? Industries want to minimize mitigation measures to maximize profits. We need to remind ourselves of God's calculus. God exalts the humble. The first will be last and the last will be first. We need to really rethink how we run our businesses with God in mind. He is not just concerned with how we treat those that work for us but also how we treat our neighbors and the part of creation our strivings affect. God can shovel blessings in faster than we can shovel them out. Am I loving God and my neighbor (including non-clients) in how I run my business? Am I caring for the creation in how I run my business? The bottom line of maximum profits is not the bottom line in God's reckoning.

PROBLEM 2: DEVELOPMENT

Of course, development is not a bad thing in and of itself. Development is an integral part of filling and subduing. Most of us are not developers. We go about our daily lives on land that is already developed, so much of what I discuss here may not apply directly to you, but you should read it anyway. It will mostly apply to those Christians who have the authority, ability, and money to develop land whether or not it's already been developed. Development means clearing and altering land for any human use, including transportation (roads, runways, railways), communication, agriculture, timber harvesting, mining, oil drilling, and residential, commercial, corporate, religious, and industrial development. If you are developing on land that was previously developed, then there is no concern about damaging a healthy ecosystem. But there is much to be said on improving the land that is already developed. More on this later. For now, I want to address those Christian developers that plan to build on undeveloped or semideveloped land which still has a fair amount of wild flora and fauna.

I can't emphasize the following enough: developers have an enormous capacity to harm the environment. They also have a great capacity to heal it. However, humanity's track record for development has historically been more destructive than constructive toward the natural environment. Yes, we have almost always landscaped developments with flowers, trees, and shrubs to beautify the area, but a proactive goal to minimize damage to the natural environment is a more recent endeavor of green developers. It is easy to see why our track record wasn't great. The costs of minimizing environmental damage during development is a spendy venture and few developers have sought that route because of the costs. However, since green development is on the rise, our track record is improving.

In the worst-case scenario, damage is done by man simply moving in and setting up shop. There may be no direct exploitation or malicious intent to destroy the surrounding environment. Collateral damage just happens because there is no forethought, planning, or effort to mitigate the negative impacts to the ecology of the area, let alone effort to enhance it. Nature is viewed as something in the way and needs to be removed for human occupation and activity. It often is viewed as a zero-sum game. We must increase; nature must decrease. In a certain sense the footprint of human development always entails subtraction from the footprint of nature. But even so, with much biblically guided planning it can result in a beautiful win-win synergy between development and nature. I will discuss in "Solutions" how development could be less destructive and more regenerative.

PROBLEM 3: HABITAT DESTRUCTION

Habitat destruction, which is too often a consequence of development, is by far the biggest problem because the destruction is broad-sweeping and indiscriminate. The people responsible are often oblivious to the ecological consequences until it's too late. Straightforward habitat destruction is pretty obvious, but the concept also includes *habitat fragmentation*. This occurs when roads or other types of development slice and dice undeveloped habitat into chunks of various sizes. If the size of the fragments is small, the roads big, and traffic fast, it doesn't take a rocket scientist to see that animal movement between fragments is effectively severed. The habitat fragments, though they may be free from direct development, slowly dwindle due to road mortality. Successful animal movement is very important to maintain the genetic health of these fragmented populations that were once interconnected. When their movement is hindered it can ultimately result in small inbreeding populations that can dwindle to nothing. When land is developed for human use, much natural flora and fauna are often eliminated in the process, so it is understandable that development and habitat destruction are thought of as synonyms. Development's reputation must change for the better.

PROBLEM 4: DELIBERATE SLAUGHTER (OR OVERHARVEST)

Inadvertent collateral damage to nature due to development is a huge problem, but deliberate slaughter is also a problem, particularly in undeveloped countries where hunting and poaching laws are poorly enforced. In the U.S. this used to be a big problem. However, with the advent of strictly enforced laws protecting threatened and endangered species, deliberate slaughter of dwindling animals and overharvest of dwindling plants has been effectively curtailed. However, there are many historical instances, here and abroad, where certain species were deliberately slaughtered or overharvested for a variety of political, social, religious, and/or monetary reasons with no regard for its continued existence or its role in nature. The examples are many, but I have listed a few below. Man has often been responsible for threatening, endangering, bringing to the brink of extinction, or causing extinction of many, many species. The activities that result in this loss are varied but they fall under two main categories: habitat destruction and deliberate slaughter or overharvest. Since we have already discussed the first, let us consider the second.

This would include poaching and overhunting or overharvesting. Many animal species have been slaughtered to extinction or to the brink of it, to satisfy some egoistic demand, be it for food, fashion (feathers or furs), social prestige, money, etc.

Whether it is was due to habitat destruction, deliberate slaughter, or a combination of the two, the following is a small sample of creatures driven to extinction in recent history: the passenger pigeon, Pyrenean ibex, Carolina parakeet, great auk, dodo, and moa. (This is true for some plant species but not to the extent it has happened to animals). Many more are driven to the brink of extinction, such as the great egret, snowy egret, whooping crane, California condor, giant panda, ploughshare tortoise, black-footed ferret, sea otter, and bison. Thankfully some of these are making a slow but sure comeback due to the hard work of conservationists. All of this destruction has happened because of mankind's global abdication of the dominion mandate. How mankind failed in each animal's plight is varied and numerous. In all these cases it is clear that sin in some form was at work: sins of commission (greed, covetousness, envy, etc.) or omission (not taking stock of our global flocks and herds the way we should).

Too often non-biologists view biodiversity conservation as a "crusade" of environmentalists, an ace up their sleeve, so to speak, to be pulled out to thwart any and all development. Our knee-jerk response should not be, "If a tree-hugging, Gaia-worshipping enviro is for it, then I need to be against it." We must not throw out the baby with the bathwater by cultivating a fervent disregard for biodiversity just to annoy the environmentalist. We must not reject biodiversity conservation because it has become their idol. "The earth is the LORD's and the fullness thereof" (Psalm 24:1). We need to step back and view biodiversity from a biblical perspective. Remember Genesis 1:31: "And God saw everything that he had made, and behold, it was very good." What God has made and called very good is not something open to reevaluation. Deliberate or not, as stewards of creation, failure to maintain the existence of a species is inexcusable in light of the dominion mandate. Proverbs 27:23–24 says, "Know well the condition of your flocks, and give attention to your herds, for riches do not last forever; and does a crown endure to all generations?"

This passage is referring to your own private flock, but since God told mankind to have dominion "over the fish of the sea and over the birds of the heavens and over every living thing that moves on the earth," in one sense all creatures on earth are mankind's global flock, mankind's global herd. Consequently, we have egregiously neglected our global responsibility, especially when extinction happens.

But what about the first part of the dominion mandate? "Be fruitful and multiply and fill the earth and subdue it . . ." You might assume that it is a zero-sum game. If we're fruitful and multiply, then that means some species might be inadvertently rubbed off the face of the earth. However, we need to obey both parts of the mandate. Having dominion over all the creatures does not mean blithely whittling away at the created diversity. God also commanded the creatures He created to be fruitful and multiply and to fill the sea and earth, not just us. We need to use wisdom and knowledge to figure out, on a global scale, how both can be accomplished. It is up to us to figure out a win-win situation where both man and creatures fill the earth while maintaining the created diversity. This will take a lot of work and co-operation between developers and ecologists. These are things developers should seriously consider doing.

1. *Design development plans, methods, and strategies (be it construction, agricultural, timbering, or mining) to minimize damage and promote healing during and after perturbation.*

    In the case of agriculture, implement methods that are regenerative (e.g. permaculture), those that enrich the soil, reduce erosion, and control pests while trying to minimize the use of pesticides. This requires homework, scientific research, and money. It means being informed on the basics of the particular ecosystem regardless of how it's used. This includes the living parts of it. Learn about and cultivate an appreciation of the plants and animals in it, particularly any threatened or endangered species. A developer needs to think like a surgeon invading a patient's body. Surgeons don't just know how to skillfully wield surgical implements. They also need to know a lot about the human body. They need to know how to plan and prepare for the operation, and they need to know how to keep the person alive during and after it. Ecosystems are much more forgiving than a human body, but they also have many working parts. Surgeons don't have to know everything and neither does a developer. However, a developer can work and cooperate with ecologists who can inform and guide him into an ecologically wise development plan to minimize casualties and disturbance to the surrounding ecosystem. The nature of surgery always involves damage to the tissues, but great care is taken to make sure the patient stays healthy and heals properly after being sewn up. In the same way, an ecosystem will be temporarily damaged, but if it is done wisely it can heal and thrive after development has occurred. With great ingenuity, it may thrive even more than in its pre-development state.

2. *Develop building plans and landscaping that architecturally harmonize with the surrounding landscape or seascape.*

I am not attempting to set out a detailed plan on *how* to do all this. That has already been done at many different scales from single residences to entire cities. Figuring out the how is not the goal of this book: that can be done by researching what green developers are doing and asking some probing questions with your biblical worldview glasses on. For starters ask yourself: What is the *best practice* for doing what I'm doing in the location I'm doing it? Am I conforming to the biblical dominion principles discussed thus far? With regard to landscaping and the design of buildings, am I thinking about how to glorify God by making everything beautiful? Are the buildings built to last so that I can bless the present generation and the generations to come? If the plans done by others aren't up to snuff, then try to glean the good stuff from them and reject any foolish stuff, such as government subsidized practices that claim to be green but really aren't. It is also very possible to find wrongly motivated environmentalists with great ideas, skill, and expertise who use their talent for the wrong reasons. No matter. Solomon used an idolatrous Gentile nation to cut and prepare timber for the house of God. Why? Because there was "no one so skilled in felling timber as the Sidonians" (1 Kgs. 5:6, NIV). Whether it's industry, commercial, or residential development, the long-term benefits of honoring God, His creation, and loving your neighbor will be a blessing to both you and the natural world around you.

3. *Don't develop everything.*

If we've figured out how to develop in a lovely way, that doesn't mean we should. Some suggest that the entire globe will ultimately be a beautiful garden-city. I hope not. Yes, cities should be turned into garden-cities. As the earth becomes full of the knowledge of the Lord, cities will become a harmonious blend of urban infrastructure and nature.[35] They will be woven together beautifully and in a way that both thrive. Ugly or hazardous pollution and waste will be a thing of the past. Any unpleasant offscouring of civilization will be incinerated or recycled and put to good use. Encouraging efforts in this direction can be seen on Singapore's Pulau Semakau. This island was a landfill made mostly of ash from the incinerated waste of Singapore. Today tropical terrestrial and marine life is abounding on and around the island.[36] It may not be perfect but it is a grand step in the right direction. We should applaud and learn from these great projects. Ultimately garden-cities will be wonderful, but that doesn't mean that every square foot of the planet should be developed into garden-cities or converted into arable land. Remember Psalm 104:16–18: "The

35. For an argument as to why this will be the case in history, see my brother's book *Heaven Misplaced* (Moscow, ID: Canon Press, 2008).

36. Linette Lai, "Semakau—not just a landfill but full of life," *The Straits Times*, October 14, 2018, https://www.straitstimes.com/singapore/environment/semakau-not-just-a-landfill-but-full-of-life.

trees of the LORD are watered abundantly, the cedars of
Lebanon that he planted. In them the birds build their
nests; the stork has her home in the fir trees. The high
mountains are for the wild goats; the rocks are a refuge
for the rock badgers." The psalmist clearly portrays a
number of wild habitats belonging to a number of wild
creatures as a good thing. He also seems to rejoice in
the fact that God made it that way and that it can stay
that way. Exercising dominion definitely entails domesticating creatures that are great for human use, but it
also entails not domesticating creatures that aren't cut
out for human use. If they don't fit into our economy,
that doesn't mean they don't fit into God's economy.
Psalms 8, 84, and 104 extol a variety of wild animals and
allude to the fact that their wild status is not something
that needs to be remedied. If you consider Behemoth
in Job 40:15–24, God is very pleased with the fact that
this wondrous beast is not subjugated by man:

Behold, Behemoth, which I made as I made you;
he eats grass like an ox. Behold, his strength in his
loins, and his power in the muscles of his belly.
He makes his tail stiff like a cedar; the sinews of
his thighs are knit together. His bones are tubes of
bronze, his limbs like bars of iron.

He is the first of the works of God; let him who
made him bring near his sword! For the mountains

yield food for him where all the wild beasts play. Under the lotus plants he lies, in the shelter of the reeds and in the marsh. For his shade the lotus trees cover him; the willows of the brook surround him. Behold, if the river is turbulent he is not frightened; he is confident though Jordan rushes against his mouth. Can one take him by his eyes, or pierce his nose with a snare?

And God speaks of Leviathan in the same way in Job 41:1–34. Read the entire chapter. The idea of taming the creature is laughable. Here is a sample:

> Can you put a rope in his nose or pierce his jaw with a hook? Will he make many pleas to you? Will he speak to you soft words? Will he make a covenant with you to take him for your servant forever? Will you play with him as with a bird, or will you put him on a leash for your girls? Will traders bargain over him? Will they divide him up among the merchants? Can you fill his skin with harpoons or his head with fishing spears? Lay your hands on him; remember the battle—you will not do it again! Behold, the hope of a man is false; he is laid low even at the sight of him. (Job 41:2–9)

In an ultimate sense they are under man's dominion, but wise dominion includes setting aside wildlands for the express purpose of granting habitat to wild animals. Their place isn't just in the zoo. Not only is wildland often the only appropriate home for many animals, virgin wilderness renews the human soul in ways that developed land, even if pleasant and beautiful, doesn't. Gifford Pinchot, Chief Forester under Presidents Theodore Roosevelt and William Taft, was stifled by the highly groomed forests of France and their overly tidy forestry practices. He and Teddy yearned for the wild forests of America. Why? It's hard to put one's finger on it. In the glorious passage in Isaiah 11:6–9 describing the eschaton, the wild creatures appear to be dwelling with some domesticated creatures and children. The wild ones will be good, not necessarily tame. I don't think the mountain of the Lord has pens, paddocks, or petting zoos. The passage in Isaiah says,

> The wolf shall dwell with the lamb, and the leopard shall lie down with the young goat, and the calf and the lion and the fattened calf together; and a little child shall lead them. The cow and the bear shall graze; their young shall lie down together; and the lion shall eat straw like the ox. The nursing child shall play over the hole of the cobra, and the weaned child shall put his hand on the adder's den. They shall not hurt or destroy in all my holy mountain; for the earth shall be full of the knowledge of the LORD as the waters cover the sea. (vv. 6–9)

PROBLEM 5: CLIMATE CHANGE

Climate change is inescapable. Since the great Flood, climate has always been changing to various degrees, for various reasons, and with good and bad outcomes. In light of the highly charged political climate there are several questions that people need to ask. 1) Is the planet really warming? 2) If it is warming, did humans cause it? 3) If it is warming, is it necessarily bad?

I have investigated these questions to my satisfaction and come to my own conclusions. I realize I don't have exhaustive knowledge. Neither do I have access to all relevant data or the expertise to analyze it completely. If you're not a climatologist then it really comes down to who you trust: "The one who states his case first seems right, until the other comes and examines him" (Prov. 18:17). In the current political climate the best way to get people to believe that man-caused climate change is a crisis[37] is to make sure nobody comes along to cross-examine it. There are many strong opinions buffeting us on all sides telling us what to think. My desire is not to tell you *what* to think but rather *how* to think. We all can use simple logic when confronted with raw facts. It appears that most people on both sides of the argument have access to a lot of the same data. This, by the way, is very similar to the creation/evolution controversy: very

37. Crisis: policies must be implemented ASAP or dire consequences will result.

different worldviews look at the same data and draw very different conclusions. The problem is finding a level-headed climatologist who interprets the data objectively without an alarmist spin. Let's consider the questions I mentioned earlier:

1) Is the globe warming? Yes, a little. Most climatologists on both sides of the debate agree that there appears to be a slight warming of about 1.3°F over the last century.

2) If it is warming, did humans cause it? The main disagreement lies in whether our use of fossil fuels (which produces a lot of greenhouse gases) is a major culprit in raising the average global temperature. Some of the sunlight entering our atmosphere is reflected off the surface of the earth as infrared (heat) radiation. Certain gases like, carbon dioxide (CO_2), methane (CH_4), nitrus oxide (N_2O), etc., have properties that trap infrared radiation which warms the atmosphere in a similar way that glass ceilings trap the sun's infrared radiation within greenhouses. Most of us know that greenhouses can be warm and balmy on a cold sunny day. This is why these gases are called greenhouse gases. Since the combustion of fossil fuels is a major contributor to the large amounts of greenhouse gases added to the atmosphere, it is assumed that they are the primary cause of this slight warming trend. According to the Climate Institute, humans have increased CO_2 levels 37% since the Industrial Revolution. Here we should be very leery and circumspect before jumping to conclusions, even if their number is correct. Yes, greenhouse gases trap heat. And yes, we have added a lot of it to the atmosphere through combustion of fossil fuels. But it is also true that there are negative feedback mechanisms, both physical and biological, that can act like a global thermostat preventing runaway warming.

Also, let's consider some other facts. 1) There is good evidence that there was a medieval warming period from about AD 900 to 1300. [38] This warming was centuries before the Industrial Revolution kicked in (which is when massive amounts of fossil fuels started being burned and greenhouse gases started to rise in earnest). Whatever the cause of the medieval warming period, it wasn't due to our collective carbon footprint. This historical fact raises considerable doubt that our greenhouse gas production (carbon footprint) is the main culprit for the slight rise in temperature during the last century. 2) If we assume that human-generated greenhouse gases result in global warming, then we should expect there to be a stronger correlation between increased temperature and increased greenhouse gas. But this is not the case. Temperature trends do not show a clear connection. The global temperatures have experienced a plateauing (global warming hiatus) between

38. *Encyclopaedia Britannica Online*, s.v. "Medieval warm period," by John P. Rafferty, https://www.britannica.com/science/medieval-warm-period.

1998 and 2012.[39] Throughout this period, greenhouse gases continued to rise. This lack of correlation reveals a lack of conclusive evidence that man-made greenhouse gases have caused the slight warming. Understanding climate change and the interplay between all the dynamic factors that contribute to it is extremely complicated. I am not saying there couldn't be a link, but if there is a link, it is certainly open to dispute. And if there is a link, it is a negligible contributor. There should be more humility among those who claim there is a clear connection. The global warming alarmists maintain a stream of rhetoric dismissing any dissenting viewpoint as anti-science, deluded, ignorant, etc. But all reasonable scientific discourse should welcome dissenting viewpoints from credentialed scientists.[40] Consensus "science," which quickly becomes agenda-driven, does not. As the saying goes: "Argument weak; shout louder." When I see how climate change alarmists adopt a condescending or dismissive attitude toward climate change skeptics, refuse to interact with reasonable counter arguments, and staunchly maintain the undeniability of the current climate crisis, I can no longer trust their word. When I do look at the data, I become even more dubious.

39. "Climate Models and the Hiatus in Global Mean Surface Warming of the Past 15 Years," *IPCC*, Climate Change 2013: Technical Summary.
40. See Judith Curry's site, Climate Etc., for a good example of strong commitment to honest data analysis among scientists: https://judithcurry.com.

3) If it is warming, is it necessarily bad? So, for the sake of argument, let's just assume it is warming because of human activity. The smart approach is always to look at all sides of the question. Don't just believe scientists who only show you doomsday computer models forecasting catastrophic consequences for life on earth. Good critical thinkers should smell agenda-driven "science" a mile away. Modeling something like climate is an extremely complicated affair and is fraught with huge levels of uncertainty. Global climate involves a long list of variables whose complex interactions and outcomes are exceedingly unpredictable. Therefore, dogmatic pronouncements about cataclysmic consequences of temperature increases are simply untenable. Let's say a local weatherperson states dogmatically that the weather in your town will be cloudy, windy, and 63°F, a month from today. We take her word with a grain of salt, and rightly so. How in the world could climate prophets be even more certain in predicting doomsday climate trends on a grander scale farther into the future? If there are high levels of uncertainty predicting local weather a month from now, then when we predict climate decades from now, there will be even more uncertainty. Alarmists often cherry-pick and highlight all the possible negative consequences of warming trends. On the other hand, global warming enthusiasts can cherry-pick the benefits while sweeping the negatives under the carpet.

If they highlight the possible benefits afforded by climate change and ignore the negatives, I wouldn't take them seriously either. Everybody has a bias, but one's bias shouldn't insulate one from honestly considering other very reasonable interpretations of the data.

Most scientists hate not knowing stuff, especially in their field of expertise. Humility in one's own discipline is rare jewel and it is quite obvious when a scientist is lacking it. When scientists are truly humble, then discussion about distant future events is always couched in qualified, non-committal language. This is not a weakness, but it can quickly feel like a weakness when the public is clamoring for clear answers from "the experts." I see the temptation to cave to the pressure when that's what the public wants, but it's still wrong to say, "Thus saith science . . ." when assumptions and conclusions are very iffy. It should be noted here that confidence isn't necessarily arrogance. Humble scientists may be confident too but only when their conclusions aren't resting on thin ice and their conclusions are not founded on spindly assumptions. In other words, confidence is in order when they have good data (all independent variables are known), it has been rigorously peer-reviewed from squinty-eyed opponents, and they scrupulously apply rigorous statistical analysis. But humility is extremely lacking in the mainstream of climate science because the public wants certainty and humble scientists refuse to deliver certainty when nothing is certain. Climate predictions for the distant future are anything but certain.

There tends to be a fixation on certain negative outcomes like rising sea levels and the inundation of large coastal cities, or desertification, or widespread famine, etc. But these outcomes are again based on models that don't have a good track record. Predictions are almost always iffy, but predictions aren't all doomsday. The alarmists have insulated themselves from all the possible benefits of global warming. Let's look at photosynthesis. With warmer average temperatures and increased CO_2 there will simply be more photosynthesis happening. By the way, photosynthesis removes CO_2 from the atmosphere, which is one of the negative feedback mechanisms contributing to our global thermostat. All in all, there will be more plant (and algal) biomass in general. More CO_2 alone may increase photosynthetic production, but it won't necessarily be high quality production if other soil nutrients are lacking.[41] We need to be holistic in our approach to plant production. Primary production will infuse more energy into many ecosystems. Provided that sufficient nutrients are available and that we maintain a high microbial biodiversity within each

41. Helena Bottemiller Evich, "The Great Nutrient Collapse," *Politico*, September 13, 2017, http://www.politico.com/agenda/story/2017/09/13/food-nutrients-carbon-dioxide-000511?lo=ap_a1.

ecosystem, the trend will be that each ecosystem will be able to support more species and greater numbers of each species.

More specifically, there would be increased plant reproduction in the Arctic tundra. The thawing of some of the permafrost would also make possible more arable land and longer growing seasons. There would be more forest growth worldwide. The marine phytoplankton at higher latitudes will flourish, which means that the oceans will support more zooplankton. More zooplankton will, in turn, support more fish, which will support more predators higher up in the food chain, including commercial fishermen.

Direct human benefits will result as well. Winter related deaths will decrease. Ice-free Arctic shipping will increase through the Northwest Passage between the Pacific and Atlantic Oceans. Many species will expand their distribution into higher latitudes. These are just a few possible benefits of modest warming and increased CO_2.

What about rising sea levels? Let's suppose there is a significant sea level increase. This is a real problem to be overcome, but consider the Netherlands. They have a country that is largely below sea level, but even so they have been overcoming this problem for centuries. Though the country is currently post-Christian, thanks to a strong historical Christian worldview that produced Western science and technology, the Netherlands is in a good position to solve this kind of problem. As necessary, they have been able to engineer solutions to rising sea levels.

The myriad humanitarian gains for human health and longevity provided by fossil fuels are clearly documented in Alex Epstein's book A Moral Case for Fossil Fuels. They far outweigh the negative impact of a modest sea level rise[42] or other supposed evils of fossil fuels listed by alarmists.[43] It's amazing how the media, steered by the scientific community, can control our attitude toward any climate trend. If they wanted to, they could launch a campaign about how wonderful global warming is, enumerating all the benefits to humanity and downplaying the negatives, and people would be rejoicing in the streets and plotting ways to make it happen faster.

Glaciers shrinking? Polar Bear distribution shrinking? Sea levels rising? Grizzlies expanding? Life finds a way. Change is the fundamental catalyst of the Darwinian theory of life! They say we evil humans are causing the change to happen too fast for organisms to adapt. According to their worldview that isn't the case. Their interpretation of earth history says there have

42. Dramatic sea level rise is very unlikely. Alarmist predictions have a very poor track record.

43. There are many benefits (energy, transportation, health, etc.) of fossil fuels that we would lose if we relied solely on alternative energy sources. See Alex Epstein, The Moral Case for Fossil Fuels (New York: Portfolio/Penguin, 2015).

been several catastrophes resulting in mass extinctions before humans were around and yet new flora and fauna evolved from the ruins. Why are they so worried? New life will evolve, right? Maybe even cooler critters than the last batch. Why do they insist that the behavior of *Homo sapiens* is unnatural if our species (and any kind of human behavior) is the result of 100% naturalistic evolution? Why have the scientific authorities decided that a particular global climate status is the best and we must do everything in our collective power to maintain the status quo into perpetuity? There may be other climate conditions vastly superior to the current one. Other global temperatures may support a higher global biodiversity and an improved human welfare than our current one. From both creationist and evolutionary perspectives, tropical and subtropical ecosystems which teem with biological life were much more widespread in the past than they are today. Why do they fear any tiny step in that direction?

PROBLEM 6: OVERPOPULATION
Ever since Thomas Malthus made gloomy predictions of human population growth in 1799, many people have believed that we have an overpopulation problem. During the sixties and seventies, when ecological concerns came to the forefront of national politics, a number of notable scholars began making spectacularly wrong

predictions regarding the global population growth of humans. Foremost among them is Dr. Paul Ehrlich, Bing Professor of Population Studies in the Department of Biology at Stanford University (author of the 1968 bestselling book *The Population Bomb*), who has repeatedly made forecasts of apocalyptic proportions. Here are a couple that should make us pause before ever taking him seriously again. This quote was from the April 1970 issue of *Mademoiselle*, "The death rate will increase until at least 100–200 million people per year will be starving to death during the next ten years." In another essay entitled "Eco-Catastrophe!" he writes, "By 1975 some experts feel that food shortages will have escalated the present level of world hunger and starvation into famines of unbelievable proportions. Other experts, more optimistic, think the ultimate food-population collision will not occur until the decade of the 1980s." Of course, his and other doomsayer predictions didn't come to pass. Curiously Ehrlich doesn't seem to back away from his extravagantly wrong predictions. He still thinks he's correct about the consequences of overpopulation, and continues to pontificate doomsday predictions about overpopulation and other ecological problems. It is time to turn a deaf ear to him.

Currently overpopulation is not the issue on the front burner of ecological problems. Climate change, habitat destruction, and extinction are the ones we hear most about. In fact, quite a few countries are expected to have a negative growth rate between 2006 and 2050 because the death rate is exceeding the birth rate.[44] Nevertheless the world population overall continues to grow, but not as fast as before. So what is the limit? Carrying capacity is defined by ecologists as the population size that can be sustained by the available natural resources, but this is a very difficult figure to determine for animals and impossible for humans. The overpopulation alarmists of today and the past have wrongly assumed that humans are like other life forms and that we simply grow logistically to a carrying capacity where natural resources can no longer sustain continued growth. The population then plateaus; this plateau is called the carrying capacity.

Though ecologists are aware of many factors that cause carrying capacities to fluctuate in natural communities, there is one major factor they overlooked in humans. This factor is our cleverness, our ingenuity, and our capacity to innovate solutions to seemingly insurmountable problems. We glory in overcoming limitations that animals can't overcome. We waltz past our supposed carrying capacity over and over. We modify the environment. We make more room by constructing taller buildings. We make more land. We irrigate dry land so food grows in places it normally couldn't. We

44. Matt Rosenberg, "Negative Population Growth," *ThoughtCo.*, February 9, 2018, https://www.thoughtco.com/negative-population-growth-1435471.

come up with countless ways to encourage the land to produce more and more food. We figure out better ways to harness energy. We figure out better ways to reduce or recycle wastes. All this is why we continually defy the predictions of the doomsayers.

I don't deny the planet has limits and humans have limits: there is some nebulous carrying capacity that only God knows. The dominion mandate says "be fruitful and multiply and fill the earth." The secular liberals are very miserly in what they call filling. They say we are either nearing our carrying capacity, at our carrying capacity, or we've already exceeded it. They point to all the bad ecological problems we are causing as evidence that there are too many of us. But the problems we cause are a function of how we disobey God, not a function of how many there are of us. I've been in homes where one kid seemed like too many and in homes of similar size with many children where the home seemed roomy and peaceful. We are far from filling the earth. I don't dispute the many egregious problems we've caused, but it's not our numbers: poverty and starvation are more often caused by wars and wicked governmental regimes, not the world's inability to produce enough food. Some areas on our globe have high densities and the standard of living is pretty high (like Fremont, CA). In other areas with equal densities, there is extreme poverty, slums, hunger, and disease (like Bangladesh). What's the difference? P.J. O'Rourke compares and contrasts these two places in *All the Trouble in the World* and shows that it isn't the number of people causing all of Bangladesh's problems. It is the difference in the prevailing religious worldviews and the type of governments that they have inherited as a result. This all affects the productivity of the citizens, the economy, the city's infrastructure, etc.[45]

We really can't calculate our carrying capacity simply because we are incapable of predicting our future innovations and future blessings. If God blesses the nations spiritually with a global revival, then God will bless the nations materially. This is something secularists don't acknowledge. Secularists think people are intelligent, highly evolved animals that have figured out how to control our destiny. They try to calculate our carrying capacity and then dictate our limits. Secularists have worked hard to take God completely out of the equation. Even many Christians are marching to their drum, especially in Europe, where much of Christianity has become the secularist environmental agenda's lapdog. It is a shame when pastors are anemic on the Gospel, ambivalent on abortion and same-sex mirage, but will thunder with conviction when preaching about recycling, reducing carbon footprints, and shopping fair trade. Our faith regarding

45. P.J. O'Rourke, and Blair Cooper, *All the Trouble in the World: the Lighter Side of Overpopulation, Famine, Ecological Disaster, Ethnic Hatred, Plague, and Poverty* (Auckland, New Zealand: Royal New Zealand Foundation of the Blind, 2013).

the blessing of God has shriveled to almost nothing. Remember, all the many physical variables that scientists study are ultimately in God's hands. God can increase our carrying capacity. He can do this by blessing man's innovativeness, changing the climate, or by decreasing the amount of tundra, deserts, and other inhospitable land. He can directly increase the landmass through volcanism or indirectly through human engineering. He can increase the productivity of the oceans by causing many more areas of upwelling.[46] Upwelling areas are currently about 0.1% of the surface of the ocean, but about 50% of the commercial fish catch come from them.[47] Just think what the productivity of the ocean would be if upwelling areas increased just tenfold.

We too often limit God's blessings to spiritual warm fuzzies. We are so anemic in our imagination, we think we are actually crowded on this planet. Have you ever flown in a jet plane and looked down? Most of the land is uninhabited or very sparsely inhabited. Even in urban areas where population density is high, lots of people in one place is never the real issue. High densities may exacerbate other problems, but it isn't the actual problem. Not to oversimplify, but sin is what causes most

46. Upwellings are currents that bring nutrients up from bottom sediments. This causes phytoplankton and zooplankton to proliferate, which in turn causes fish to proliferate.
47. George Karleskint et al., *Introduction to Marine Biology* (Belmont, CA: Brooks/Cole, 2013).

of our problems. Ungodly governmental systems like socialism and communism set off a domino effect of ever-increasing human misery. More and more people become lazy. The incentive to work in a nanny state diminishes with time. Consequently unemployment, depression, divorce, suicide, alcoholism, sex addiction/trafficking, and many other social and spiritual ills snowball into more misery and less productivity. The cumulative effect of this is the dissolution of adequate infrastructure, resulting in horrid waste management and wastewater treatment, open sewers, dilapidated everything, squalid living conditions, rats, disease, etc. Other nasty outgrowths of many sinful people in urban settings are godless education, corruption, gang warfare, injustice, high crime rates, etc. It is worth noting that people everywhere are sinful, both in urban *and* rural settings. Even capitalism and free markets where greed is unrestrained can also cause many problems, but the system provides some measure of checks and balances. In this case, covetousness and greed are the problem, not capitalism or free markets. The only problem with city densities is that when you concentrate people, you concentrate sin. It is then easy to commit the fallacy of guilt by association and throw the baby out with the bathwater. We blame the high density of people as the problem rather than the high density of sin. It is easy to blame squalid living conditions, corruption, disease, malnutrition, etc. on a huge population because there is a strong correlation between the two in many instances. And when there is a strong correlation, it is easy to make the claim that huge populations are the problem. But correlation is not the same thing as causation: we need to look for other factors that might be the real problem. The slums of Sao Paulo, Brazil; Mumbai, India; and Dhaka, Bangladesh are horrendous examples of what false religion and bad governmental systems plus high densities can look like. Fremont, California and Singapore also have very high densities, but because there is a sound infrastructure and decent rule of law that rewards productivity and punishes crime, these cities thrive. I am not saying Fremont and Singapore are cities burgeoning with believers, but insofar as they abide by some semblance of Christian-based rule of law, high density cities can be places of peace and prosperity rather than hovels of broken infrastructure, corruption, malnutrition, and disease, all made worse by high population.

But even cities that seem to have it together can come under the judgment of God. God made the world in such a way that we reap what we sow. The more a community abides by the law of God at least externally, the more it will function properly in peace and prosperity, and the environment will be healthier. When a large percentage of people in a municipality love their neighbors, they are more concerned about keeping their air, food, and water breathable, eatable, and drinkable. There will always be agendas to improve everything from construction of buildings and landscaping of city parks and other green space to waste management. Loving God and your neighbor at a community level will always improve a municipality in very tangible ways. Conversely, the more a community deviates from the law of God, the more you will see a downward spiral towards a dystopian society.

In this lengthy chapter we discussed a number of environmental problems: pollution, development, habitat destruction, deliberate slaughter, climate change, and overpopulation. Though alarmists can exaggerate problems or make nonproblems into problems that doesn't mean there aren't real problems that need addressing. Even the nonproblems need addressing because policy decisions addressing nonproblems can adversely affect whole societies. In summary, our approach to all of these should be, "What does the Bible tell me to do that actually applies to these problems?" With regard to pollution, development, habitat destruction, and deliberate slaughter, two commands come to mind: love God and love your neighbor. In loving God, you will love what He loves and value what He values. That includes biodiversity. Wild and domestic animals will be well managed and maintained. In loving our neighbor, we look out for our neighbor's welfare. Obeying these commands as far as it depends on us will make us seek to reduce pollution and will make development a much less destructive affair. In the long run, development done rightly will contribute to making beautiful garden-cities. I don't think climate change and overpopulation are real problems. Nevertheless, loving God and our neighbor at the individual level is always the first step in solving any real or perceived problems. Any positive effects of our obedience will be commensurate with the number of people loving God and their neighbor. If we want to see a reduction in the severity of these problems at the societal level, then that number needs to increase. And that is only possible through the Gospel of our Lord Jesus Christ.

DISCUSSION QUESTIONS

1. What are the six major environmental problems (most legitimate; some not) we face today?

2. Briefly summarize a biblical approach to solving each of these (if they are a real problem).

13. ROOT CAUSES, ROOT SOLUTIONS TO ENVIRONMENTAL PROBLEMS

No important change in ethics was ever accomplished without

an internal change in our intellectual emphasis, loyalties,

affections, and convictions.

ALDO LEOPOLD[48]

IF WE BELIEVE THE SECULAR AGENDA about the various causes of our environmental problems, we will be much more amenable to their proposed solutions, whether it be electric cars, solar power, wind energy, etc. Of course, many of the solutions are perfectly reasonable and deal with problems in a very straightforward way. Don't pollute the air. Don't pollute the

48. A *Sand County Almanac*, 246.

water. Don't litter. Minimize damage to habitat when developing land. Maintain biodiversity. Check.

In this chapter I would like to briefly address certain green agenda solutions like alternative energy sources (i.e. wind and solar power) to point out that they really aren't solutions. They contribute to the problem and are a major distraction away from real problems and real solutions. We are constantly told that producing more CO_2 rather than less is a flagrant sin against the environment. Environmentalists and their disciples view people who dislike wind and solar farms and who aren't falling all over themselves in an attempt to reduce their carbon footprint the same way the Pharisees viewed tax collectors. They set up the antithesis like this: *We environmentalists are conscientious souls that want to save the earth; all others are callous and are destroying it for selfish gain.* Not only is it wrong-headed to view CO_2 as a bad gas, the solutions to replace icky fossils fuels are not so green at all!

Consider wind farms. Huge tracts of land dotted with many tall, white excrescences are not only an eyesore to most folks, but they are not even economically sustainable. They are a continual drain on the taxpayer due to their reliance on government subsidies.[49] These

49. Robert Bryce, "Wind-Energy Sector Gets $176 Billion Worth of Crony Capitalism," *National Review*, June 6, 2016, https://www.nationalreview.com/2016/06/wind-energy-subsidies-billions/

wind turbines are extremely expensive to make and maintain, and they simply can't pay for themselves. The mining for their materials and their manufacture is also damaging to the environment. Wind energy is intermittent, and is not very abundant, cheap, or scalable (capable of being easily expanded or upgraded on demand). If stored, it must be stored with enormous batteries, and the process of making these batteries is not healthy for the environment either. If the users paid the actual costs for this kind of energy (cradle to grave[50] costs without any government subsidies) it simply would not be affordable. Even if everyone liked how they looked, the fact that it's a burden to the taxpayer in perpetuity is plenty reason to end the foolishness now. Apart from their lack of aesthetic appeal and apart from being a drain on the taxpayer, they take up a lot of habitat. The moving blades are a real, though small, hazard to bats and birds. Measures are being taken to minimize this hazard, but these measures increase the cost. Sound vibrations of these blades cutting through the air are a source of sound pollution and are off-putting to wind farm neighbors. Efforts are being made to minimize this as well, in keeping with "good neighbor" practices. However, efforts to minimize a variety of unpleasant effects caused by a totally unnecessary alternative energy is not neighborly at all.

50. *Cradle to grave* means from creation to disposal.

If a private landowner wants to put up his own wind turbine (and can pay for it himself) to power his household because he's crunched the numbers, it's cost effective, and it's aesthetically pleasing to him, then God bless him. Wind energy is not intrinsically wrong, but because of its reliance on subsidies, its poor scalability, its low reliability due to its intermittent nature, and low density, this energy source is a silly choice economically for entire cities. The secular agenda has managed to impose a less green alternative by demonizing fossil fuels. They then deceive the public about how green their alternative is.

Solar farms, though very different, pose similar problems. They are not cost effective. Even in Phoenix, Arizona where it is sunny most of the year, solar energy, if all costs are considered, is not breaking even, let alone making a profit. The cradle to grave environmental impact of solar energy is no trivial matter. Mining hazardous minerals for the photovoltaic (PV) cells and manufacturing, installing, and disposing of solar panels involve a number of hazardous chemicals and care must be taken to ensure that these chemicals are handled, transported, and contained in ways that are safe to people and the environment. As is true for wind farms, solar farms also take up a lot of real estate, mostly arid and semi-arid habitat. Birds and insects are fried if they fly through concentrated beams of sunlight emitted from solar power towers.

Despite all these negatives, the green agenda is fairly effective in concealing the unseemly side of green energy. Unless you are deeply committed to the erroneous belief that reducing carbon emissions will halt climate change and save the earth's inhabitants, the extremely high cost of wind and solar farms demanding government subsidies, coupled with habitat loss, wildlife mortality, and handling/disposal of hazardous chemicals, means it's simply not worth it.

As I have mentioned before, the root cause of all evil, death, grief, and futility is the Fall of Adam and the sinful nature all humanity inherited and participated in. Romans 6:23 makes it clear: "For the wages of sin is death, but the free gift of God is eternal life in Christ Jesus our Lord." Romans 8:20–22 also mentions that the Fall didn't just have spiritual consequences:

> For the creation was subjected to futility, not willingly, but because of him who subjected it, in hope that the creation itself will be set free from its bondage to corruption and obtain the freedom of the glory of the children of God. For we know that the whole creation has been groaning together in the pains of childbirth until now.

There can be a direct link or an indirect link between our sinfulness and environmental problems. An example of the former is simple greed for plumage or pelts resulting in the extinction of some bird or beast. The indirect link is not empirically provable, but is still very clear in Scripture. In many texts in the Old Testament, God strikes the land with a curse due to the sins of the nation of Israel. We often don't speak of these curses in terms of ecological catastrophes because biblical language doesn't use words like environment or biodiversity, but if you examine these curses, they mostly involve God chastising the children of Israel where it will hurt the most—the environment. Let's start with Deuteronomy 28:15–24:

> But if you will not obey the voice of the LORD your God or be careful to do all his commandments and his statutes that I command you today, then all these curses shall come upon you and overtake you. Cursed shall you be in the city, and cursed shall you be in the field. Cursed shall be your basket and your kneading bowl. Cursed shall be the fruit of your womb and the fruit of your ground, the increase of your herds and the young of your flock. Cursed shall you be when you come in, and cursed shall you be when you go out.
>
> The LORD will send on you curses, confusion, and frustration in all that you undertake to do, until you are destroyed and perish quickly on account of the evil of your deeds, because you have forsaken me. The LORD

will make the pestilence stick to you until he has consumed you off the land that you are entering to take
possession of it. The LORD will strike you with wasting
disease and with fever, inflammation and fiery heat,
and with drought and with blight and with mildew.
They shall pursue you until you perish. And the heavens over your head shall be bronze, and the earth under
you shall be iron. The LORD will make the rain of your
land powder. From heaven dust shall come down on
you until you are destroyed.

Look closely at the nature of all these curses. God
ends the productivity of the land through drought, resulting in famine. He increases human and agricultural
diseases. The diseases involve God controlling microbial
activity in the environment. We've imbibed too much
secular thinking when we factor God out of climate, soil
health, and population dynamics of disease-causing microbes. Practically speaking do we think more like naturalists, or do we really believe God is exhaustively in
control of the environment?

Ezekiel 14:21 says, "For thus says the Lord GOD: How
much more when I send upon Jerusalem my four disastrous acts of judgment, sword, famine, wild beasts, and
pestilence, to cut off from it man and beast!"

Note that out of the four disastrous acts of judgments,
three are environmental crises, i.e., famine, wild beasts,

and pestilence. Again, it is clear in Scripture that these disasters are not just random events in nature happening apart from God's will. They can be traced back to the Author of life judging the sin of His people. When one of these occurs, that doesn't necessarily mean that the people, city, or nation are worse sinners than another (Lk. 13:4). Nevertheless, it can be an act of judgment. Amos 3:6 says,

> Is a trumpet blown in a city,
>> and the people are not afraid?
> Does disaster come to a city,
>> unless the LORD has done it?

Just because natural disasters are a form of judgment on a people or a nation doesn't mean each person that suffers from it is guilty. Righteous people in the Old and New Testaments suffered frequently through drought and famine. Hosea 4:1:1–3 says,

> Hear the word of the LORD, O children of Israel,
>> for the LORD has a controversy with the inhabitants
>>> of the land.
> There is no faithfulness or steadfast love,
>> and no knowledge of God in the land;
> there is swearing, lying, murder, stealing, and commit-
>> ting adultery;

they break all bounds, and bloodshed follows
bloodshed.
Therefore the land mourns,
and all who dwell in it languish,
and also the beasts of the field
and the birds of the heavens,
and even the fish of the sea are taken away.

In verses 1 and 2 Hosea tells the children of Israel
God's grievances against them. He specifies the sins He
is dealing with: Swearing, lying, murder, stealing, adul-
tery, general rebellion ("break all bounds"), and lots of
bloodshed. Verse 3 tells us the consequences of committing these sins:

Therefore the land mourns,
and all who dwell in it languish,
and also the beasts of the field
and the birds of the heavens,
and even the fish of the sea are taken away.

One of the best ways God gets our attention when
we rebel is to make the land mourn (all languish; birds,
beasts, and fish are taken away). In other words, God
causes some kind of environmental disaster. A bountiful land allows us to wax fat and kick. Though this
has happened countless times in the Old Testament

and throughout world history, we still haven't learned this lesson. Our collective sin is what provokes God to chastise us with environmental disasters, not our carbon footprint.

This kind of judgment is not limited to the children of Israel for breaking covenant. It applies to us in the new covenant. Paul comments on this in 1 Corinthians 10:6–12:

> *Now these things took place as examples for us, that we might not desire evil as they did. Do not be idolaters as some of them were; as it is written, "The people sat down to eat and drink and rose up to play." We must not indulge in sexual immorality as some of them did, and twenty-three thousand fell in a single day. We must not put Christ to the test, as some of them did and were destroyed by serpents, nor grumble, as some of them did and were destroyed by the Destroyer. Now these things happened to them as an example, but they were written down for our instruction, on whom the end of the ages has come. Therefore let anyone who thinks that he stands take heed lest he fall.* (emphasis added)

That said, we conservatives need to sober up and stop gloating over the false warnings and alarms of the environmentalists. Yes, they may exaggerate our various problems or prioritize them wrongly. They may even point at some problem when it really isn't a problem, or they may even be wrong about the cause of a real problem. However, we too often smugly laugh at them because they are oh-so-wrong. However, with over 61 million abortions performed in the U.S. since *Roe v. Wade*, rampant divorce, sex trade, pedophilia, pornography, transgenderism, and same-sex mirage, to name just a few, I am confident that God is not happy with this country. I may disagree with how secular environmentalists have assessed our environmental problems, but when I think of the sinfulness of the U.S., we deserve far worse than the gloomiest doomsday predictions of the most angry, spittle-flecked environmentalist.

So what is the solution? Better environmental legislation? More environmental activism? More electric cars, solar panels, wind turbines, etc.? The solution is much simpler, yet not physical or tangible, and addresses the root of the problem: sin. If sin—not just original sin from Adam, but our ongoing participation in his sin—is the ultimate cause of all environmental problems, then the solution to those problems is the solution to our sin, which is the Gospel: the death, burial, resurrection, and ascension of the Lord Jesus Christ and the command to believe in Him. Whether individual sins or corporate sins, Jesus is the only solution that gets at the root of the problem. We die in

Him, we are buried with Him, and we are raised with Him. Our sins have been washed away, and the Holy Spirit gives us a new heart, and a new desire to please God in our thoughts, words, and deeds. The transforming power of grace at the personal level, which is multiplied in the Great Commission, begins to solve many other problems at a larger scale, both cultural and environmental. Remember the yeast and the loaf. Never say, "What can one microscopic yeast cell do to a whole lump of dough?" When we pursue new legislation, recycle, think warm fuzzy thoughts about the environment, start a new organization to deal with one of our environmental messes, it really isn't addressing the root problem.

As Francis Schaeffer drives home in *Pollution and the Death of Man*, "If I love the Lover, I love what the Lover has made."[51] This is true, not just in our thoughts and feelings, but also in our actions. When I'm reconciled to the Creator, it follows that I will be reconciled to the creation. You've heard the saying, "Ideas have consequences"? Well, salvation has more. Salvation doesn't just change our thinking: it is the first step toward transforming and renewing our minds and our hearts and our actions. When we are reconciled to our Creator, we begin to love what He loves. He loves our neighbor and He gives us grace to do the same. He said His creation

51. Page 93.

is "very good," and our evaluation should be right in line with His. Through the process of sanctification, the Spirit conforms us to the image of Christ, and our thoughts, words, and actions become more and more like the Lord Jesus Christ. Yes, the creation is fallen, but so is mankind, and we are not called to plunge mankind into further ruin. Rather, we are called to be couriers of the Gospel, agents to bring salvation to the world. The redemption of the creation parallels the redemption of mankind. Again, Isaiah 11:9 says,

> They shall not hurt or destroy in all my holy mountain;
>   for the earth shall be full of the knowledge of the LORD
>   as the waters cover the sea.

Notice that when the knowledge of the Lord has filled the earth as extensively as water covers our oceans, our relationship with our fellow creatures ceases to be adversarial. I think what annoys many folks about environmentalists is how they seem to be only concerned about the damage humans are doing to the environment and the living things within it, but fail to see how much damage is done in the other direction. The glorious thing about this passage is that both parties "shall not hurt or destroy." The cessation of conflict is a two-way street. Not only will we stop destroying our fellow creatures, fellow creatures will stop destroying each other and us. It's worth reading again:

> The wolf shall dwell with the lamb, and the leopard shall lie down with the young goat, and the calf and the lion and the fattened calf together; and a little child shall lead them. The cow and the bear shall graze; their young shall lie down together; and the lion shall eat straw like the ox. The nursing child shall play over the hole of the cobra, and the weaned child shall put his hand on the adder's den. (Isa. 11:6–8)

In this wonderful passage we see that the end game is the end of adversarial relationships. We should seek solutions to move in that direction God's way, but for now, your job may be one in which some or most of your time and energy is spent protecting humanity from the ravages of living organisms.[52] That means you're a professional hitman for certain plants, animals, or microbes, and that is a worthy pursuit in a fallen world. However, we need to get better at minimizing collateral damage to innocent parties. That means fighting the cussedness of certain creatures and cultivating the blessings of others. The former includes

---

52. This isn't an exhaustive list, but these general areas are enormous and probably cover most of our conflicts with troublesome microbes, plants, and animals: pest control from fleas, lice, and rats in urban settings, to aphids to elephants in agriculture settings (this could also include predators of livestock and humans), and snake bite treatment and disease control in the medical, veterinary, and agricultural sciences.

redeeming harmful creatures by discovering their pre-fallen role in nature if possible, and restoring them to it.

The greatest commandments are to love the Lord God with all our heart, mind, soul, and strength and to love our neighbor as ourselves. As we obey the Gospel in its fullest sense, God will eventually redeem the creation. He may bless it miraculously but He often blesses through ordinary cause and effect, as manifested through our innovations, ingenuity, and hard work under the lordship of Jesus Christ. Whichever way God brings it to pass, this glorious state of affairs will come to be.

So what can we do if God is pleased to use us as means to His ends?

THE GOSPEL AND ACTIVISM

I've already stated that the Gospel is the ultimate solution because it accomplishes much more than forgiveness. The Holy Spirit comes in and regenerates everything; Jesus Christ is Lord over everything—our heart, mind, and actions. That's why I've never been keen about activism as a solution. Activism consists of vigorous campaigning to bring about political or social change. It is all about external political coercion, while the Gospel is about internal transformation. Secular environmentalists often want to effect change through activism. Even if they have admirable goals like biodiversity conservation and succeed in affecting some change, it generally just spurs into action those who essentially agree; it normally doesn't change the minds or hearts of those who don't, and it usually exacerbates the polarization that already exists. Activism may influence those on the fence who already have a soft spot toward nature, but if you tell Anti-green Andy that the Feds want to save this or that plant or animal, what's the first thing Anti-green Andy wants to do? If you don't change the hearts of the people who don't share your values, then law enforcement is the only way to get them to conform. That requires stiff penalties to create disincentives. It also requires enough law enforcement officers to bust folks who don't comply. All this costs more taxpayer money to pay for something they don't value, polarizing them even more. It's frustrating, expensive to the taxpayer, and increases tensions and hostilities between interest groups. So that's why I think it's not very effective to impose a large number of environmental policies on a chafing public. Of course not everyone will have a change of heart and govern themselves correctly, and therefore there will always be a need for good environmental laws and adequate enforcement to get people to abide by those laws. Some people require coercion to do the right thing, like "Don't poach" or "Don't pollute" for fear of a stiff fine if caught. Christians should obey the laws of the land because of conscience, not just because of possible punishment

(Rom. 13:5). Nevertheless, I'd rather spread the Gospel and let it do the changing of hearts. It may not happen overnight, but there will be a gradual cultural transformation. Again, as Schaeffer put it, "If I love the Lover, I love what the Lover has made."[53] The Gospel is the only way I can begin to love the Lover. This is the best way.

But what if you don't need me to convince you to love the creation? Let's suppose you want some specific marching orders. Here are some tangible things you can do to facilitate this at the grassroots level.

FOSTER AN APPRECIATION OF NATURE: ADOPT A HOBBY

Plunge yourself into a hobby that involves learning about some group of animals, plants, etc. As you immerse yourself into learning about that group, whether it's birds, reptiles and amphibians, trees, wildflowers, mushrooms, etc., your love of creation will at least be enhanced. This can be contagious too. If you're not obnoxious in your enthusiasm, your friends and family may get hooked. If your kids experience your hobby as something that enhances your relationship with them, they will be all in. If it's a source of tension and competition for your time, drop it or change the way you do it. If you're a biology teacher, spread enthusiasm to your students, not just information. As a biology professor at New Saint

53. Schaeffer and Middlemann, 93.

Andrews College, I'm very keen to take my classes on field trips. Whether it is herpetology, marine biology, entomology, botany, or ornithology, there is nothing that generates an interest, appreciation, and enthusiasm of God's creation more than getting students immersed in the outdoors. I don't want field trips structured in a dour Captain von Trapp style. I'm excited to be outside and eager to explore and discover anything related to the course, which tends to be contagious. The students have course requirements to meet, but they also have a long leash. I want their time in the outdoors to evoke worship. I want them to be caught up in childlike wonder as they experience the beauty and goodness of the creation. A quote from *Redeeming Creation* captures it well:

> Modern worship must return to an emphasis on the joy of the works and wonders of God in order that joy may become once again an experience instead of a concept. Joy must be a taste, a touch, and a smell, not an idea only, and God must be not only the Lord of heaven above but also the Maker of earth beneath. Until these practices find their place in right worship of God, it is not to be wondered at that our devotions are insipid, our prayers bland and our state of mind a million miles

from the "joy unspeakable" described in Scripture as
the proper state of Christians.[54]

Whatever group of living things you like best, get a
good national or regional field guide and any basic par-
aphernalia needed (camera, binoculars, field journal,
etc.) and find fellow Christians with the same interest.
It's so much better to learn ecology in the context of
something you already enjoy. If a nature society has mis-
sions and goals not in conflict with Scripture and you
can in good conscience join, do so. You'll learn more
from seasoned naturalists than you could on your own,
plus you'll meet plenty of non-Christians who may be
shocked that a Christian is in their midst.

If you hunt, be an informed, circumspect hunter.
Learn the ecology and natural history of your quarry.
It will give you a deeper appreciation of the animal,
because you'll understand to some degree its role in
nature, not just how much freezer space it will take up.
You'll learn what it needs in terms of habitat and resources to sustain a healthy population into perpetuity.
Presumably, as a hunter, you would want your descendants to be able to enjoy the sport as you do. You can
also influence the hunting culture beyond family and
friends. One of the earliest conservation societies in

54. Fred VanDyke et al., *Redeeming Creation* (Downers Grove, IL: Inter-
Varsity Press, 1996), 37.

the U.S. was the Boone and Crockett Club.[55] Members included hunters like Teddy Roosevelt and Gifford Pinchot, and they were definitely keen on conserving wildlands and its natural inhabitants while still enjoying the sport. The great conservationist and author Aldo Leopold sums up this mindset well after describing the wonderful sky dance of the woodcock in *A Sand County Almanac*:

> The woodcock is a living refutation of the theory that the utility of a game bird is to serve as a target, or to pose gracefully on a slice of toast. No one would rather hunt woodcock in October than I, but since learning of the sky dance I find myself calling one or two birds enough. I must be sure that, come April, there be no dearth of dancers in the sky.[56]

As a Christian, you can in good conscience make a point of learning about some aspect of nature. The more you study nature, the more you appreciate its beauty, complexity, and diversity. Appreciation in turn causes you to value it. And what you value, you naturally desire to conserve. When there is enough people that really want it conserved, then top-down command and control from some State or Federal regulatory agency

55. See Boone and Crockett Club, http://www.boone-crockett.org/.
56. Leopold and Schwartz, 36.

need not impose some environmental law. When people are governed internally there is less need to impose environmental policy externally. Unfortunately, too many people do the easiest thing, the most entertaining thing, or the thing that maximizes profit without regard for their surroundings or future generations. The only thing that will stop this selfish mindset is strong Gospel preaching. It's not only about forgiveness of sins. The Gospel is bigger than that. It transforms every facet of our life. Everything (heart, mind, and soul) should be in complete submission to the lordship of Jesus Christ. It transforms our lives, our relationships, our culture, and our environment.

ENCOURAGE YOUR CHILDREN'S LOVE OF NATURE

If you're a parent you probably know that kids naturally like nature. Encourage it! Too many tidy parents extinguish this innate desire by being overly fastidious about their pristine home decor, and they freak out when various critters show up unannounced after a child's ramble in the woods. Perfectionist moms and dads need to learn to encourage and accommodate this innate love of nature. This may involve garter snake husbandry, tadpole rearing, or insect collecting. You're welcome to maintain house rules of cleanliness, but don't act like it's the Holy of Holies. Never avoid learning about nature when confronted with real nature. A bucket of tadpoles is a better way to learn about the frog life cycle than an encyclopedia entry. Embrace it, welcome it, and cultivate the love that's already there. Remember, God said "it was very good."

GET YOURSELF IN THE GREAT OUTDOORS

To really get to know and appreciate the great outdoors at the gut level, there is nothing better than immersing yourself in it. This can include hunting, fishing, camping, boating, hiking, gardening, etc. Take your pick . . . or not. As my brother and pastor says, it's a *get to*, not a *got to*. Christians are very prone to feel false guilt for not doing something a Christian pastor or author says is a good thing to do. So if you're inclined, go for it; if not, don't. Foster and cultivate outdoor activities that you already enjoy. Don't just do it as a box to check to assuage false guilt. If uneven ground, dirt, insects, or temperatures above or below 72°F is a major hardship, then I suggest you wade in from the shallow end. If what I've mentioned so far is too ambitious for your preferred existence of filtered air, flat floors, and fluorescent lighting, then try the following.

VISIT ZOOS AND STUFF

Even indoorsy people enjoy seeing living animals and plants. If you're in that camp, make a habit of visiting zoos, aquaria, botanical gardens, and parks. Most of these have really improved a lot over the last several decades. You don't even have to get hiking boots. Most of the unpleasantness of the outdoors has been removed, and it's quite enjoyable. Stretch yourself. The more you see and learn, the more you'll appreciate nature. But if you consider yourself a lost cause, at least do it for the children. The concrete hasn't set with them. If the doctor ordered you to stay inside, at least watch nature documentaries. You need to see God's artwork somehow.

RESTORATION AND CONSERVATION

This requires some serious involvement. Various Christian environmental organizations like A Rocha[57] have trained professionals overseeing and directing volunteers who want to work in the trenches on clearly defined local conservation projects, whether it be restoring degraded habitats, helping the poor, conservation of endangered species, etc. They also want to get their hands dirty alongside other Christians who want an outlet to

57. Kelli Mahoney, "8 Christian Environmental Organizations: Coming Together to Be Stewards Over the Earth," ThoughtCo., March 6, 2017, https://www.thoughtco.com/christian-environmental-organizations -712499. Disclaimer: I can't personally vouch for each of these organizations mentioned here. You'll have to do the homework yourself like Bereans to see if their mission and goals have a good understanding of Christian dominion or if some have been overly influenced by the secular environmental agenda.

serve God in this area. Some might say that these efforts are a case of getting our priorities mixed up. Why should a Christian work to restore a degraded wetland when there are countless degraded people who need the Gospel? True, people need the Gospel, but the Gospel can be proclaimed from countless occupations. It is clear in Scripture that Christians can have many different lawful interests and callings. To exercise your calling to the glory of God is pleasing and honoring to Him. The Gospel isn't just the spoken truth about the saving power of Jesus Christ; it is the saving power of Jesus Christ lived out in a joyful, obedient Christian, regardless of his or her occupation. One lesson the Reformation taught us, is that every lawful calling for a committed Christian is full time Christian work.[58] It's not a matter of choosing between Christian ministry or reclamation ecology; Christian ministry or airline pilot; Christian ministry or physician; Christian ministry or homemaker. For committed Christians, it's not what you do that determines whether you are in full-time Christian work: it's how you do it. "And whatever you do, in word or deed, do everything in the name of the Lord Jesus, giving thanks to God the Father through him" (Col. 3:17).

DISCUSSION QUESTIONS

58. See Gene Edward Veith's *God at Work: Your Christian Vocation in All of Life* (2002; Wheaton, IL: Crossway, 2011).

1. What are the two main alternative energy sources promoted today by the green agenda?

2. What probing questions should one ask about any energy source that is being foisted on the public as a solution to an environmental problem?

3. What is the root solution to all environmental problems? How so?

4. Discuss some the practical ways we can foster an appreciation of nature in ourselves, in our families, and in our churches (without it becoming a chore).

14. HOW SHALL WE NOW LIVE?

Christians, of all people, should not be the destroyers. We should
treat nature with an overwhelming respect. We may cut down a
tree to build a house, or to make a fire to keep the family warm.
But we should not cut down the tree just to cut down the tree.

FRANCIS A. SCHAEFFER[59]

SO, WHAT DID I WANT TO ACCOMPLISH
in this book? As you can see, I didn't lay out specific
marching orders for every conceivable profession that re-
lates to the natural world. That would require many vol-
umes and many writers who have much more expertise
in all those professions than I do. Rather, this is a book
seeking to apply biblical principles to the living creation.
I hope that many believers who read this book will see

59. *Pollution and the Death of Man*, 75.

the biological world not as the domain of secularists, nor simply as an apologetic tool promoting creationism, but rather as their Father's world, a world made by a Father who loves it and created it brimming with biological diversity, a world over which our Father commanded us to exercise dominion, biblically understood. We have, in the main, made a hash of it. We need to take a hard look at what we have done, and we need to strengthen what we've done right and learn from what we've done badly, even when God-denying earth-worshippers point it out to us. We must always have our Bible open because some of their accusations are simply false. Sometimes they call a foul when there really wasn't one. But some of them are true. That's why we need to marinate in God's Word so we can discern what is right and wrong regarding everything.

Although I'm not an expert in all the areas that need our attention, I love the creation because I love God. I want my fellow believers to have a desire to do the same. Then I want the experts to figure out how these principles can be applied in their particular vocations. You may be a conservation biologist bringing endangered species back from the brink of extinction. You may be a CEO of an industrial paper mill. Your profession may be at cross purposes to the job of a fellow Christian, and it's hard to think how you could not be at each other's throats, but with God all things

are possible. If you and someone else have opposing
attitudes regarding the dominion mandate, both of
you first need to love each other. You must walk in
the light and be in fellowship with each other or you
won't get anywhere. Think through the issues (don't
emote), pray for wisdom, let your gentleness (reason-
ableness) be obvious, and read your Bible daily. Put all
your biases and assumptions on the chopping block of
Scripture. We will never come to unity on dominion
issues if we stubbornly adhere to entrenched attitudes
that have been dear to vocations on either end of this
spectrum. Anti-green Andy attitudes die hard: "This
is the way we've always harvested timber, disposed of
waste, cleared land, and I ain't gonna change!" They
do need to repent of this attitude. On the other side
of the spectrum, extremely unbiblical, secular environmental ideologies have seeped into many undiscerning
Christian noggins. They also need to repent of any left-
ist notions that don't square with Scripture, particularly the idea that *Homo sapiens* is a virus and that the
world would be a better place without our species, or
that CO_2 is an evil gas. Both extremes are wronghead-
ed. Christians should first earnestly try to apply these
biblical principles to their own behavior and their own
job. As the Scripture says, first remove any logs from
your own eye before attempting to do eye surgery on
your brother.

By God's grace, Christians who work toward seemingly different goals can start seeing the lawfulness of other professions. As I mentioned earlier, ecologists should work with developers. In an ideal situation, a Christian ecologist should recognize that a Christian developer can develop to the glory of God. A Christian developer should appreciate the diversity and vulnerability of the wild native plants and creatures on the land he is going to develop and should seek out ecologists who could help draw up a plan to minimize damages and facilitate recovery of the disturbed areas, ideally because he wants to, not because he's forced to.

The State can only try to curb our destructive behavior assuming the State can identify the problem in the first place. At best the State can only put a Band-Aid on the gangrene. The ultimate problem that threatens the welfare of this wonderful creation is the collective sinfulness of mankind. The ultimate solution is our Savior and Creator, Jesus Christ (Jn. 1:1–3). The reality of His life, death, burial, resurrection, and ascension is the only thing that deals decisively with our sins and reconciles us to God the Father. Once that occurs, we can begin to exercise wise dominion under His lordship and begin to heal the damage our sins have wrought on the creation.

DISCUSSION QUESTIONS

1. How should we treat the biological creation in light of what we've learned about the dominion mandate?

2. How should we approach other Christians with attitudes and actions that are contrary to the ideas presented in this book?

3. Describe ideally how ecologists and developers should work in harmony. What would happen if one was calling the shots without the other?

FURTHER READING

(Be a Berean; hold everything up to the standard of Scripture.)

- *Pollution and the Death of Man*, by Francis A. Schaeffer
- *Redeeming Creation*, by Fred H. Van Dyke, David C. Mahan, Joseph K. Sheldon, Raymond H. Brand
- *Where Garden Meets Wilderness*, by E. Calvin Beisner
- *A Sand County Almanac*, by Aldo Leopold
- *Hard Green*, by Peter Huber
- *A Moral Case for Fossil Fuels*, by Alex Epstein

ACKNOWLEDGMENTS

I sincerely thank my friend and colleague Mr. Peter Escalante for encouraging me to write this book after hearing me give a presentation on the topic. I also am grateful to my British son-in-law, Dr. Daniel Newman, for prodding me at every opportunity to write this book. Lastly, I thank my dear wife, Meredith, who is my ever-present cheerleader, motivating me to stay the course. Her example of cheerful diligence coupled with her Tigger personality helps me reach the finish line with joy.